The Only Writing
Series You'll Ever Need:
Screenwriting

Insider tips and techniques
to write for the silver screen!

Madeline DiMaggio

Adams Media
Avon, Massachusetts

Contains portions of material adapted or abridged from *The Everything® Screenwriting Book*
by Robert Pollock, © 2003, F+W Publications, Inc.

Published by Adams Media,
an F+W Publications Company
57 Littlefield Street, Avon, MA 02322
www.adamsmedia.com

ISBN 10: 1-59869-288-7
ISBN 13: 978-1-59869-288-4

Printed in Canada.

J I H G F E D C B A

Library of Congress Cataloging-in-Publication Data
available from the publisher

Contents

Introduction

Film is a visual art form. It can entertain without words but it can't exist without pictures. Writing the screenplay requires more than just literary skills; it requires the writer to think in images instead of words. In film you "*show*" instead of talk about, you "*indicate*" rather than explain. It is an art of less. Unlike the novel, the script is not "complete." It is a series of visual impressions giving the illusion of completeness. In film and television the visuals always move the action forward. In film the writer must think in pictures. The goal of the script is not to get it sold, but to make it a good read. Narrative and locales come alive in the reader's head so they can envision the movie. There is powerful plot progression, attention-grabbing turning points, and a strong beginning, middle, and end. The reader is compelled to turn the page. The script transports them, time passes, and they're not even conscious of it.

Crafting a good script is a creative challenge for the novice as well as for the veteran writer. Over the last twenty-five years I have written over forty hours of produced television and film in just about every genre: sitcoms, hour-action, hour-drama, pilots, animation, soaps, documentaries, movies for television, and feature films. Every script is different; each has its own set of problems and tests your grit. At times I've asked myself, "how come this hasn't gotten any easier?" One time I got so stuck I had to look in a book I wrote to see what I had to say about it! I've threatened to quit, and yet I can't seem to stop writing. I've cursed the industry, but I can't seem to leave it. Someone once said Hollywood is an asylum where the lunatics are terrified of being let out. That said, film is the most exciting and powerful medium in existence. I can't even talk about a great movie without getting chilled to my bone. Careers in this industry are like roller coasters, but the freedom to create, the thrill of bouncing ideas off creative minds, the joy of newness with every project, and the excitement of seeing your work on the screen has been worth it for me. Some people regret having been faced with the same unknowns, the continual rejections, the flux of income, writing in hopes of a sale, but if you asked me if I would do it all again and I wouldn't even blink before I answered yes.

I believe the craft of television and movie writing *can* be taught, but the passion that carries you along is another thing. I had a student named Kevin Falls who wrote seven screenplays before he even got an agent. At a conference once a writer asked him, "how did you keep going?" Kevin said he asked himself the same thing, "what if I never sell a screenplay?" His answer was, "it doesn't matter, I love it so much I'm going to keep writing anyway. I believe Kevin's perseverance is what determined Kevin's outcome. He went on to become an Emmy Award–winning writer and the executive producer of *West Wing*.

As a teacher I have had the great fortune of watching screenwriters evolve. But I have learned over the years that it's not always the most talented who make it, it's the ones who love it so much that they keep trying.

I love writing, I feel passionate about it. I love going to the movies and I love watching good television. I once asked a group of 200 "want to be" screenwriters, "How many of you have completed a script?" At least half of the people in the room raised a hand. Then I asked, "How many of you have sold a script?" Only one hand was raised. I then asked "How many of you regret having written?" Not a single hand in the group went up.

My goal is to provide you with the screenwriting tools that can lay the foundation for your success. This is an A to Z in scriptwriting; how to think in pictures, the devices scriptwriters use, how stories develop, the hooks that grab an audience, great characters, the art of dialogue, and most important, basic screenplay structure. There are insights into the industry from writers, directors, and brilliant creative minds who will offer you strategies and tricks of the trade. Most important, I hope you will enjoy yourself along the way.

Chapter 1

Here's Your Cue!

The Bare Bones: What Is a Screenplay?

A screenplay or film script is a blueprint from which, eventually, a motion picture will be made. This blueprint is the most important element of a film—you can't produce a film without a screenplay just as you can't construct a skyscraper without architectural blueprints. A screenplay is what the musical score is to the symphony, what the human skeleton to is to the body. It is the bare bones and without it there would be nothing. Essentially the screenwriter provides everything—every time you write the dialogue you are the actor, every time you create the locale you are the director, every time you cut between the scenes you are the film editor. The scriptwriter provides the bare essentials, and hopefully well enough to attract other creators who will bring their special talents to the project.

But Without YOU, the Writer, There Wouldn't Be a Movie!

When actors, directors, cinematographers, and editors get up at the Oscar podium to give their thanks for their awards, they often thank the scriptwriter, without whom they wouldn't be at the podium.

Likewise, without the great talent they bring to the written word there would be no award-winning movie. This all goes to show that film is a highly collaborative art.

Great Screenplays in the Past

Think of the great screenplays over the years. They almost all had great directors, actors, editors, music scores, and production people who attached their incredible talent to the projects. Recently the Writers Guild of America came out with a list of the 101 greatest screenplays ever written. Although not in any particular order, here are some of the most recently written ones:

- *Shakespeare in Love* by Mark Norman and Tom Stoppard
- *American Beauty* by Alan Ball
- *Fargo* by Joel and Ethan Cohen
- *Jerry Maguire* by Cameron Crowe
- *Thelma and Louise* by Callie Khouri
- *The Shawshank Redemption* by Frank Durabond, based on a story by S. King
- *Field of Dreams* by Phil Alden Robinson. Based on a book by W. P. Kinsella
- *Back to the Future* by Robert Zemeckis and Bob Gale
- *Sideways* by Alexander Payne and Jim Taylor
- *The Sixth Sense* by M. Night Shyamalan

Not a Sure Deal

Unfortunately, it doesn't follow that a fine screenplay is all that's needed. Without naming names, there have been examples of films with great scripts, phenomenal casts, plus award-winning directors, cinematographers, and editors that have bombed not only with the critics but at the box office. On the other hand, there have been

※ See ˄movies that are highlighted (or watch again)

pictures that started off looking as if they would be a disaster on all fronts but turned out to be classic successes. It's a matter of fitting the pieces of the puzzle together.

From Script to Successful Motion Picture

Although most scripts are written by only one person, it requires hundreds of professionals to make a script into a film. To organize the venture, the project must have a leader. In the movies, this is the role of the director. Really, you and your screenplay are just the beginning. But in essence, you have much of the power!

The Screenwriter Plays God

Which of the platoon's heroes will die? The comic who is always cracking jokes, the serious lieutenant who always worries about his family back home, the unrelenting sadistic sergeant who is ready to lead his men into battle? It's up to the scriptwriter; he or she is the one who plays God, deciding for a variety of dramatic reasons who lives or dies.

Writer Beware!

The cinematographer, sound designer and engineer, set and costume designers, editors, composers, musicians, and others working on film production generally receive a copy of the script of the movie they are working on.

The scriptwriter might write a close-up: Slowly the dismembered hand moves and rejoins its wrist. The tendons, muscles, and, finally, the skin are miraculously healed and the hand and arm look as they used to be. Then the scriptwriter will save that text and go to lunch. Months later, a special effects computer technician will spend hours creating the effect that eventually audiences will gasp at. That's what the business of movie writing is all about.

"It Takes a Village…"

A film is rarely the product of one person. If you have the opportunity, pay a quick visit to a film set, and you'll see how many people it takes to work on the shooting. Although it's hard to admit, it isn't always easy for a creative individual to work as part of a team. Have you ever heard of an artist who shared the credit for his painting with others? No great painting was ever made by a team. Even in literature, few writers collaborate on novels and even fewer co-write poems. But for you, the reality is that your idea and creation will have to be shared and worked on by dozens—or even hundreds—of people.

Hit Trick

"Tell me a story! Because without a story, you are merely using words to prove that you can string them together in logical sentences." —Anne McCaffrey, American science fiction author best known for her Dragonriders of Pern series.

There's No "I" in Team

In the ideal situation, the film production team relies on the script written by one screenwriter and makes minimal changes to your vision of the film. However, in many instances this isn't the case at all. Sometimes, it's hard to say where parts of the movie came from. Consider the problem of writing a good ending. Did you know that the ending of *American Beauty* was redone after it was viewed by a focus group? In fact, many movies have endings that weren't in the screenplay at all.

Probably the most famous case of a "Who came up with the ending?" mystery in film history is the ending of *Casablanca*. As you probably remember, Ilsa goes off on the plane to Lisbon with her husband, Victor Laszlo. Rick shoots Major Strasser, then Rick and Captain Renault watch the plane as it leaves; then they go off into the fog with the famous last line from Rick: "Louis, I think this is the beginning of a beautiful friendship." But who came up with that ending?

Casablanca was written by Howard Koch and the Epstein twins. Apparently, it was more or less written on the fly, which often meant it went from the typewriter to the set. It's a Hollywood legend that an ending hadn't been decided on until right up to the last days of shooting. Even then, three or more versions were written and shot until the filmmakers made their final decision.

The possible candidates for writing that final ending were the Epstein twins, Howard Koch, and Casey Robinson, who collaborated in one way or another in writing the screenplay; Michael Curtiz, who directed the film; and Hal B. Wallis, the film's producer. In spite of all the excellent books on the making of *Casablanca*, the closest one can get to the truth is that the last line was an off-the-cuff last thought from producer Wallis. But even that can't be verified!

So what can we learn from the *Casablanca* tale? The scriptwriter should enter the fray recognizing that he or she is a member of the team and won't always be the last authority on making decisions. Sometimes, the director or the producer will decide to change the ending, the actors may choose to say their lines differently than how you had intended, and the cinematographer may prefer different shots than the ones specified in the script. This lack of control is something you should be prepared to accept as part of the filmmaking process.

From Toddler to Titan: A Screenplay's Growth

So, is what you sit down to write exactly what gets distributed on the set? Not really. You write a screenplay and you send it to an agent or producer for consideration. If the screenplay is accepted and plans are made to shoot the film, your screenplay will be modified into a "shooting script," or scenario. By the time a director and actors see the screenplay, it is in the form of a shooting script.

Hit Trick

"When I sit at my table to write, I never know what it's going to be until I'm underway. I trust my inspiration, which sometimes comes and sometimes doesn't. But I don't sit back waiting for it. I work every day." —Alberto Moravia, one of the leading Italian writers in the twentieth century.

The shooting script retains all of the information included in the screenplay, but it goes into much greater detail. In other words, the shooting script has all the dialogue and description plus extensive technical notes like various camera directions.

Most often, the director or director's assistant will include the directions, like CUT, C.U., PAN, ZOOM, and so on. Beginning writers love to insert those directions into their screenplay, thinking that it makes the screenplay look more professional, but don't do this because it actually creates the opposite impression. Unless you are specifically writing a shooting script, leave the detailed directions alone.

Most shooting scripts have the scenes numbered and rearranged in the order in which they will be shot—not necessarily the order of how the movie will be put together. So, if you need to film two scenes at the same location that are supposed to take place six months apart, they may appear together in the shooting script. For example, let's say at the beginning of the movie the hero is standing outside the law courts in London, waiting for a woman. Six months later, he's back at the same location, this time with a different woman. In spite of the time difference, those two scenes would be numbered sequentially and would be shot one after the other.

"I'm Writing a What?": A Screenplay on Spec

Unless you are preparing a shooting script for a film that's in the works, what you are writing is a "screenplay on spec"—a screenplay that hasn't been commissioned. You are submitting it unsolicited in the hope that the producers will be impressed by your writing and the idea, and will make you an offer for your screenplay. Or you may submit it to an agent, who'll meet with producers on your behalf.

Writer Beware!

The production manager is a key person on the set. He or she is the producer's representative and is the behind-the-scenes team player who is in charge of running the show. In most cases, the production manager is responsible for authorizing payments and paychecks.

What you have to be sure about is that you have not submitted a shooting script. Many writers go to the extent of writing in all sorts of instructions that shouldn't be there. It would be very useful to remember that the writer's job is to tell the story; it is the director who is responsible for the look and manner of the way it's told.

You will find books on bookstore shelves subtitled *The Shooting Script*. Actually, that's generally incorrect because it's not a shooting script at all. The average reader wouldn't be able to make head nor tail of a shooting script with all its scene numbers, directions, and odd pagination, with scenes in no apparent order. Your spec script is something different and should be an easy read for any reader, in the business or not. Never be put off by simplicity; in fact, aim for it every time.

Remember this!!!!
(Does NOT have to be complex!)

Chapter 2

Crafting Reality

Idea-lly, You've Been Brainstorming

What specifically makes a movie, or gets it off the ground? The answer is almost too simple to believe: an original idea. Another way of saying "idea" in the business is "concept." You are going to hear those two words and the Hollywood meaning behind them time and time again. Remember them, they're important. It's funny to think of it this way but the last step in writing the screenplay is actually writing! Hard thought and a lot of preparation happen even before you are ready to begin stepping out the story. How do you come up with an idea worthy of transforming into a movie? Maybe it just happens. Ever heard the phrase that the best ideas can come in the shower?

It may be true for you, or an idea may dawn on you while you are out fishing, driving, watching a movie, or doing any other activity that isn't at all related to writing or consciously thinking about writing. Sometimes, the key is to stop thinking hard and let the ideas come to you.

Intuition, which in this context is another word for inspiration, can play a great role in creation. Learn to trust your gut feeling! The more you trust it, the stronger it will tend to become.

Writer Beware!

Sometimes writers become overly involved in creating a film related to a current event or trendy topic. They get so tied up in it being contemporary that they forget that even if it were bought right now, it would take at least a year or more to get to the cinemas. By then the chances are that "timely" would have lost its attraction.

Finding Inspiration

All writers should look at human nature, both historically and currently, and absorb from it as it suits his or her creativity. Remember that right from the beginning of the creative process we are heavily involved in the subjective—subjective not only in terms of opinion about our own work and the work of others, but in our selections as they are exhibited in the choice of what we want to use, either directly or indirectly. Generally, you will write as you are and that's exactly how it should be!

What you pick to write in your script will, particularly at the beginning of your writing career, come from your subjective viewpoint. The great writer Willa Cather wrote, "In the beginning, the artist, like his public, is wedded to old forms, old ideals, and his vision is blurred by the memory of old delights he would like to recapture." You should operate with an open mind, this way you are capable of seeing all points of view. This mindset will help you distinguish the subject from the object.

Picture Your Audience (even if they're in their underwear!)

As you think about your film idea, you need to envision whom it is you will be writing for. Think about your target audience and what their experiences and expectations may be.

When the audience gets comfortable in a cinema, all ready to see the new Julia Roberts film, for instance, it is a reasonable assumption that they are aware of what they're in for. Invariably, there have been pages and pages of advertising and reviews of the picture to prime them. In addition, they are fans of Ms. Roberts and she rarely lets them down. In exactly the same way, an audience knows how films move along; whether they are informed about film production or not, they know there will be a beginning, a middle, and an end (most prefer happy endings).

Knowing What It Takes

I believe there are four ways to learn about writing screenplays:

1. Go to the movies and rent DVDs.
2. Read produced screenplays. (It is very easy to download free scripts.)
3. Go to seminars, read books, take workshops, and WRITE!
4. Make it your job to know the industry.

The top-grossing domestic blockbusters of all time are as follows: according to the MovieWeb site, as of 2006, in descending order:

1. *Titanic*
2. *Star Wars*
3. *Shrek 2*
4. *E.T. the Extra-Terrestrial*
5. *Star Wars: Episode 1*
6. *Pirates of the Caribbean: Dead Man's Chest*
7. *Spider-Man*
8. *Star Wars Episode III: Revenge of the Sith*
9. *Lord of the Rings: The Return of the King*
10. *Spider-Man 2*

A quick look at the titles will tell you these are huge budget films. If you understand the industry and how it works, you will know big-budget blockbusters are written by A-list Hollywood writers. The A-list means top grossing screenwriters and they are a very elite handful. Trying to break in with a script that requires big special effects and a massive budget is suicide. Why? Because you will be writing yourself right out of the market. The vast majority of filmmakers and producers who buy scripts simply could not afford to make your movie. Keep this in mind when you're thinking about the scale of your screenplay, a *Titanic*-like film will be a tough sell.

Writer Beware!

They say the Western is dead. But Hollywood tends to be cynical, so you never know. The writer/director most recognized as the last Western creator of merit is Sergio Leone of **The Good, the Bad, and the Ugly** fame. His finest production is said to have been **Once Upon a Time in the West** with Henry Fonda as a sadistic killer and Jason Robards, Claudia Cardinale, and Charles Bronson.

Dare to Bare: Personal Touches

Most writers find out early on in their careers that they have a feeling for a certain kind of story. Try to follow the principle that what you love doing, you do well, because it will probably lead you in the right direction. If you absolutely love action books and action films, then maybe that's what you should write. If you are a mystery fan, maybe a film noir is the thing for you (keep reading for film noir definition). If you're interested in historical romances, why not use what you already know to write a screenplay?

Although it may seem like everything has been done before, it hasn't, not *your* way. The way you write will be a reflection of who you are, everything that you are. The sum of that will become the basis of your style. The most important element is that you have strong feelings for the subject matter you intend writing about. It helps to have passion for your subject matter, story, and characters, it will show in the end!

Time and Place

Once you've pinpointed your interest, also consider the timing and place of the story. These factors can have tremendous influence, mainly on the sales potential of the screenplay. If a budding screenwriter has become obsessed with figures of historical significance, for instance, some lower-class, little-known fellow who led a devastating charge on the British troops in one of their former colonies, he or she will have a more than difficult job convincing a studio to even take a look at the outline. The leading reason for rejecting such a project would be the thought of its budget.

Hit Trick

"Find what gave you emotion; what the action was that gave you excitement. Then write it down making it clear so that the reader can see it too." —Ernest Hemingway, an American novelist, short-story writer, and journalist.

Historical subjects are not popular with the film industry anymore. Just imagine the cost of all those costumes, let alone the locations with their castles, drawbridges, and horses.

It is a truism that if a studio can find a good reason for rejecting a screenplay, they'll find one! This is because of the vast number they receive. It is important, then, for screenwriters to choose their subject matter wisely. The possible cost of the project should be a major consideration. Make sure to think it through, and you'll be fine.

The Inner Purpose of a Screenplay

In the end it shouldn't matter which of the suggested ideas/concepts you pick to work from; there is usually more to the finished screenplay product than just a wide-ranging category title. In all matters of written creativity there is at the base of the endeavor the need to comment on the human condition.

This doesn't mean that you all of a sudden have to become a new-age scriptwriter. Two people falling in love and then falling out of love, how that happens and how they deal with the problem—that's part of the human condition just as much as any situation might be. The scriptwriter creates characters and allows the fates to throw them together, just like in real life.

Research Your Domain

To be a successful screenwriter, you have to immerse yourself in movies, learning everything you can about the way they are written and made. Quentin Tarantino, the director of *Reservoir Dogs* and *Pulp Fiction*, which in 1994 won him an Oscar for best original screenplay, did his research by working in a video rental store. The influence from the videos he must have seen can be identified in his work. For instance, *Reservoir Dogs* draws inspiration from Stanley Kubrick's *The Killing* and Martin Scorsese's *Mean Streets*, among others. An even more successful director, Steven Spielberg, spent his formative years directing TV's *Marcus Welby, M.D.,* and *Columbo* instead of going to college, learning by experience.

Hit Trick

"I would never write about someone who was not at the end of his rope." —Stanley Elkin, an American author of extravagant, satirical novels.

What's Your Type? Genre

Movies, like books, are slotted into categories or genres. We attribute the concept of genres in literature to the Greek philosopher Aristotle, the author of *Poetics*. Although it was written many centuries ago, *Poetics* has had great influence over the development of Western literature and the way we categorize it. *Poetics* is actually about writing for the theater, which was invented by the ancient Greeks. In *Poetics*, Aristotle theorizes that all theater productions may be divided into tragedy, comedy, and epic.

From this ancient idea, the movie industry has expanded into many more genres as well as subgenres. The basic film genres are:

- Action/adventure: *Pirates of the Caribbean*, the *Indiana Jones* series
- Comedy: *Something About Mary, Meet the Fockers*
- Crime: *The Godfather* movies, *Ocean's Eleven*
- Drama: *Brokeback Mountain, A Beautiful Mind*
- Epic: *Titanic, Lord of the Rings*
- Horror: *The Exorcist, The Ring*
- Juvenile: *Willy Wonka and the Chocolate Factory, Stuart Little*
- Musical: *Moulin Rouge, Chicago*
- Science fiction: *Minority Report, X-Men*
- Thriller: *A History of Violence, The Manchurian Candidate*
- War: *Saving Private Ryan, Jarhead*
- Western: *Unforgiven, Butch Cassidy and the Sundance Kid*

Choosing Your Genre

It's a good idea to decide where to sow your idea. It helps to establish, at the beginning, what genre you're going to work with. What might work well in a comedy could ruin a drama. When thinking about a category, think of what is appropriate for it—even matters like a typical budget will make a difference. Obviously, an action film generally requires a bigger budget than a comedy.

To help you get creative with choosing a genre, think of subgenres. For example, what is the subgenre of *Butch Cassidy and the Sundance Kid*, any of *The Lethal Weapon* pictures, and *Thelma and Louise*? They are all "buddy" movies. Or, think of a subgenre and then list the first three films that come to mind—that will help you figure out which films fit best into a particular category.

The Film Noir

Once you pick a genre, really get into it! Try to figure out what film was the first of its kind and how the history of that genre developed. Let's take the example of film noir. The genre emerged after World War II and featured films that were dark mystery stories. A strong element of the film noir genre has always been cynicism; generally, film noir themes are downbeat and film noir characters are brooding, dark personalities with an undercurrent of moral dignity under a hard shell. I once asked a famous writer what his definition of film noir was and he said very simply, "You get screwed!" Some examples of film noirs are:

- *Body Heat* by Lawrence Kasdan
- *LA Confidential* by Brian Helgeland and Curtis Hansen
- *Sin City* by Robert Rodriguez

Flesh It Out: The Concept

Once you've got your idea, you'll need to flesh it out into a concept, which is basically a fancy word that refers to a film idea description that will help you sell the screenplay. You will often hear the word "high concept." There are four key elements in high concept, they are:

1. A great title
2. A fascinating subject
3. A very strong hook
4. A broad audience appeal

In addition to these four elements, if your story cannot be described in a couple of short simple sentences, it is not high concept. An example would be:

- *The Hand That Rocks the Cradle*: the babysitter from hell.
- *Armageddon*: A killer meteor threatens Earth.
- *Splash*: A man discovers he's in love with a mermaid.
- *Lethal Weapon*: An officer about to retire is teamed up with a crazy suicidal cop.

The "Meets" Line

A popular way of creating a concept is to do it with the "meets" line, a log line and pitch hook that includes the word "meets." The "meets" line can help you instantly accomplish, capture, and convey in just a single line of words the concept (idea) of the proposed film.

On the face of it, a hook or "meets" line may seem pretty silly, even for Hollywood. However, surprisingly they can sum up, by presenting a mental image that is already in the mind of the reader, just what the film is about. But BEWARE, never use the "meets" line with archaic films, movies that did not do well at the box office, or generally, something silly. Let's say a screenwriter tells you that his new idea is Calamity Jane meets King Kong. From that simple phrase, you'll probably get an instant image of dear Doris Day in her cowgirl outfit with a stuffed gorilla on top of the Empire State Building. This will guarantee no one will want to hear the rest of your story let alone read it. Cutesy does not work!

A number of years ago I sold a screenplay with Pamela Wallace, Academy Award winner for the movie *Witness*. Our script was based on the book *Catherine Called Birdy*. It was about a sassy teenager in the Middle Ages who methodically rejected every suitor her father brought to her. We sold the concept as *"Shakespeare in Love"* meets

"Clueless." Both movies were big successes and set the tone for our script. The producers got it.

Film Length

The average film today is somewhere around 120 minutes long. The reason most films are 90 to 120 minutes long is very simple: People have to sit still to watch, and in our day and age most people don't have a long attention span. If you make the movie too long, your audience may lose interest. Another reason is economics—the longer the film, the more money you will need to produce it. Yes, big movies run long these days, but new writers trying to break into the business will not sell them. These scripts are written "in house." "In house" means inside the studio or production house where writers are paid to develop ideas and write scripts.

Today, unfortunately readers in Hollywood are not willing to read fat scripts from unknowns. If your screenplay runs over 117 pages they assume the writer does not know what they are doing. Scripts today are coming in leaner and leaner. I get nervous when mine exceed 112 pages and I begin doing some serious editing. I recently completed a horror script that runs 98 pages. So the popular phrase "short and sweet" applies to all writers trying to break into the industry!

Chapter 3

Writing Your Treatment and Synopsis

Intro to Treatments

Both treatments and synopses are written in narrative prose and tell the story of the screenplay. There is usually confusion about how the two differ. It is often a matter of semantics. If you are asked to submit one or the other, get clear with the person who is requesting it. Ask them flat out what they want from you. I have learned that this step can save lot of time in the long run.

In my professional experience treatments always go into more detail than a synopsis. For example, I recently had a project optioned by a producer on the Laurel Clark story. Laurel Clark was one of the female astronauts who died aboard the space shuttle Columbia. I got the rights to her story and two producers optioned it. The term "optioned" means that a writer gives up the rights to his/her script for a limited period of time, either six months or a year, for someone else to exclusively market it and hopefully ensure a sale. The synopsis ran a page and a half. Now the producers have requested a treatment that will be much more detailed and broken down into acts. Essentially they want the whole story told in narrative prose before I take on writing the script.

Hit Trick

There is no assigned length for a synopsis, but avoid overwriting. Put yourself in the place of an average agent or producer. Most of them are busy people. It's unlikely they'll want to bother with reading anything that's more than a few pages long.

New writers should concentrate on writing a good synopsis because it will inevitably be requested, but the detailed treatment is more for your sake. It is a blueprint of your story, a map that tells you where to go in executing the script. Without it, you risk running into major problems as you write.

Writing a Synopsis

A synopsis needs to tell the overall story of the film quickly and concisely. Writing it will help you solidify your story, and later you can use it as a marketing tool.

Many new scriptwriters hate writing the synopsis because tight and concise writing can be difficult. But don't drop this step because if you cannot define your story on a single page you are not ready to begin writing it! Think of it this way: without it, you risk running into major problems as you work on your screenplay.

But there's a bit of bad news here, until you have a track record, it's very unlikely you will sell an idea using either a synopsis or treatment. All producers today, if taking a chance on a novice scriptwriter, want to see the fully executed screenplay. They may request the synopsis but that is only to take a quick look at the storyline to see if they are even interested. Producers don't buy ideas anymore. They want to see how the idea is executed.

Know Whom You're Writing For

As you begin your synopsis, keep in mind your audience—this isn't your average moviegoer, but the agent or producer reading your treatment. Although you may not think it, knowing whom you are writing for gives you an element of power. You are the wielder of the words and it is the words that are going to influence the reader, so choose them carefully.

Keep in mind that your target audience is the decision makers who receive scripts in great numbers every week. Look in any of the reference books relating to agents and you'll see that they all say that they reject about 98 percent of everything they receive! Your synopsis is the first sample of your writing. It is also the pitch for your script, so it is crucial it is presented professionally and in a clear and tight fashion.

Writer Beware!

Although literary ability is not required talent for screenplays, it is for treatments, which is one reason, perhaps, that many scriptwriters don't like writing them. Most people short on writing talent, or new to it, overwrite. It is essential that treatments are well-paced, clear, and easy to read.

The Synopsis Marketing Tool

Go to your local Blockbuster, take a latte with you and spend an hour or two reading the backs of DVDs. Obviously these are marketing tools. Do they entice you to rent them? What works for you, what doesn't? What triggers an idea? In the same way your synopsis should entice agents and producers to want to read the script. It is a marketing tool. Be prepared to invest a fair amount of time and energy into this very important simple page. Do not let its brevity fool you; less is more and is often much harder to write. You will find it is a tremendous drawback to any presentation, written or made in person, if your synopsis or pitch sounds flat; enthusiasm is essential. As Ralph Waldo Emerson said, "Nothing great was ever achieved without enthusiasm."

Third Person, Present Tense

The synopsis should always be written in the third person (he/she/they) and in the present tense (now)—the advantage of writing in the present tense is its immediacy. Generally, you should avoid including direct dialogue in your treatment.

Not everybody is adept at writing in the present tense. This is mainly because most of us are used to writing in the past tense. The past tense comes easily to us all, and we've been using it for most of our lives. Using the present tense is a conscious literary device.

To help yourself become more comfortable with using the present tense, always keep in mind that you are writing for the movies and what the audience sees on the screen is what happens in front of the camera. Even if the scene takes place in the eighteenth century, the scene is being shot in the present. That's how it will be written in the script, and that is how treatments and synopses should be written.

Hit Trick

Here's how you would use third person/present tense writing in the mode of a treatment to describe what happens in Fargo: A car salesman in a Minnesota backwater hires a couple of lowlifes to kidnap his wife so that his wealthy father-in-law will pay ransom big enough to get him out of trouble. They pull it off, but during a drive in the snow at night they just happen to commit three murders. The bright police chief, who is very pregnant and speaks in a slow sort of Norwegian-type accent, investigates . . . .

Avoid Author Intrusion

There's something in narrative prose called "author intrusion" and it's not good! It happens when the author gets into the act and starts being a nuisance, either by over explaining or by telling the readers how they should feel. Even bestselling authors do it. However, in a treatment it's an absolute no-no.

Here are a few examples of the "author intrusion" type of writing that might be seen in poor character thumbnail sketches:

- The hero is this fantastic stud.
- He makes an amazing jump you wouldn't believe.
- The heroine was abused by her father.
- She's a closet lesbian.

If your short synopsis sounds like that, it's likely that you'll get a quick rejection—no explanation needed. The author should never be present in the narrative, so always stay out of sight. Show, don't tell.

It is always better not to tell the reader how characters feel; if you describe the actions of the characters, the reader will understand without being told. Always remember, your synopsis is designed mainly to create anticipation in the reader. There are no hard and fast rules but since it is only on one sheet, make it good.

The Main Text and Example

There are all sorts of opinions about how a synopsis or treatment should look. Forget any frills or tricky stuff: no colored paper or odd-looking fonts. Use 12-point Courier font. And keep the page looking clean. Here is an example of a synopsis I sent to my agent for marketing purposes. The script has since been optioned.

Undercover White Trash
Writer: Madeline DiMaggio

Place contact information here

An elitist NY ad man blows a multi-million-dollar campaign for a wholesale consumer chain. His penance is to go undercover to study his target consumer group: the blue-collar society he abhors.

This is very much in the tone of **Liar Liar**.

Synopsis

Edward Prescott the III is in trouble. He blows the ad campaign for the Billy-Mart wholesale warehouse chain and Big Billy Barnes, the wholesale King of the Southwest, threatens to take down Edward's entire company unless "the little Peckerwood," can turn it around.

Forced now to go undercover to better understand his target audience, Edward decides to machete his way into wholesale consumerism like Jane Goodall trekked into Tanganyika. Taking on his task like an anthropologist, he makes his first entry, says good-bye to all "lifelines" and dives head first into the world of trailer parks, stock cars, Southern rock and fish sticks.

While making observations in a Billy-Mart warehouse, Edward spots his perfect target family, The Fulmers, Mama, Papa, and their children, the "Five Horsemen of the apocalypse." Edward follows the Fulmers home to the Seventh Heaven mobile park and the next day rents a trailer across from them. When he discovers that Papa Fulmer is into stock cars, Edward buys a 1969 Chevelle dirt-tracker with straight pipes, wide tires, and painted with a cherry-bomb luster, and wins him over. So begins Edward's entree into the world of "deep friend and double-wide" and meeting the beautiful Gretchen, the manager of a garden shop, who will change his life forever.

The Necessary Elements

After reading the short synopsis of *Undercover White Trash*, what kind of information do you have? As you can see, this synopsis conveys a tone. It is a comedy, but there are many types of comedy. The reference to *Liar Liar* suggests that it is broad comedy, which lends itself to physical humor. Edward, the protagonist, is mentioned on the first line and clearly drives the action forward. The script has a star driven, male protagonist, as did *Liar Liar*. This is an important selling point. Although it is suggested that Edward finds love and there is a romantic aspect to the script, this is not a romantic comedy. It is a theme driven comedy. The hook of this story is Edward passing himself off as blue collar. Had I come in with the romance first it would have changed the entire tone of the read.

Writing the Treatment

The simplest way to write a treatment, after you've written a synopsis, is to follow the synopsis form but flesh it all out. A detailed treatment may be as long as thirty pages, so when you start writing the screenplay, you won't have to begin from scratch. Again, the treatment should not serve as a marketing tool and should not be submitted in place of a script unless it is requested, but it is a useful tool for the writer. The more thorough the treatment, the easier it is to write the first draft.

Treatments that are requested by producers and buyers usually only happen when the writer has enough credits to sell an idea. The presentation treatment is tough to write because it has to read with tone and emotion and be as clean as an article for *Esquire* magazine. Unlike a synopsis, a treatment is presented with a cover page, the titled centered with the writer's name directly underneath. Contact information goes on the lower left hand side of the page.

Writer Beware!

The way your work is prepared and submitted is very important. The material should give the impression of professionalism and that means no spelling or gross grammatical errors. It should look as if you know what you're doing. Even though the content of your work is what will sell it, the way it's presented is vital.

For me, writing a presentation treatment is difficult and not very enjoyable, but having produced I know why producers insist on it. It is important to know every element of the storyline and make sure the structure works before they commit the writer to script.

A Purposeful Step

When students ask me to explain the difference between a synopsis and a treatment I like to use an example from *Karate Kid*. I use the pivotal scene where Daniel's mother discovers his black eye. In the synopsis mom would simply discover his big shiner. In the treatment the question becomes how does she discover it? What is she doing? What is he doing? Where are they? What does Daniel tell her to cover up the real reason. Treatment expands on the conflict and fleshes out the details. Even with a detailed treatment it is important to remember there is no superfluous narrative—every word has a purpose. Most importantly, and this is vital in both a treatment and a synopsis, the reader should be able to "see" the action as it happens.

Chapter 4

Staging Your Screenplay

Break It on Down: Three Main Acts

We owe much of what we know about constructing screenplays to the same man who taught us about genre, Aristotle. The philosopher was born in a place called Stagira in Greece in 384 B.C.E., which places him over two thousand years back in history but his lasting influence on film creation is clear. In 350 B.C.E. he wrote a work called *Poetics*, which has influenced the structure of plays—and then screenplays— for hundreds of years.

Hit Trick

"The plot, then, is the first principle, and as it were, the soul of a tragedy; Character holds the second place . . . . Thus tragedy is the imitation of an action, and of the agents mainly with a view to the action." —Aristotle, an ancient Greek philosopher and writer.

One of his theories was that a story should be written in three acts, because every story should have a beginning, middle, and an end. And this is true of most films today. In fact, each of the acts is allotted a specific amount of time.

Act 1: The Act of the Setup

In the half-hour comedy the setup runs one to two scenes. In the hour show, three to four scenes. We now look at the movie as a two-hour unit of action. There is much more to establish here. The story is more complex and the characters have not been set. How long do you think the setup runs in the two-hour genre?

It takes twenty to thirty pages, i.e., twenty to thirty minutes—all of act one to be complete. To review, just as in the half-hour and one-hour scripts, the setup establishes the main characters and the circumstances surrounding the story. It supplies us with everything we need to get the story going like the following things:

- The tone, the texture, and the place of the movie.
- The main players.
- The problem for the main character and his or her dramatic need.

At the end of this twenty-five-page to thirty-five-page unit of action, a turning point is introduced into the story that totally shifts the action around, and throws us into Act 2.

Act 2: The Act of the Confrontation

In a film, the confrontation is a forty-five-page to sixty-page unit of action. It is here that the character meets the majority of obstacles. As the act progresses, a problem or problems are resolved, but these lead to greater complications. The second act will do the following things:

- It presents obstacles to the character's dramatic need.
- Creates the rising conflict and action of the script.
- Raises the stakes for the character.

At the end of the confrontation, another turning point occurs that turns the story around and catapults the action into Act 3.

Act 3: The Act of the Resolution.

The third and final act in a film is the resolution, a twenty-five-page to thirty-five-page unit of action. It is here that the story builds to a climax and is resolved. Act 3 is interesting because:

- It presents a moment of discovery and change for the character.
- Builds toward the climax.
- Allows the character to achieve or not achieve his or her dramatic need.
- And resolves the story (usually in the last three to five pages of the script).

The Subplot

The purpose of a subplot is to provide new interest and add more substance to the plot, in particular to the lengthier and more eventful second act. The subtext is literally what happens underneath the text. That is, it's the thoughts and motivations that are never directly expressed by the characters.

For example, let's say you write a romantic comedy with a basic three-act structure:

1. Boy meets girl.
2. Boy loses girl.
3. Boy wins girl.

The subplot may be an added story. Let's say the male protagonist has trouble at work and is falsely accused of embezzlement. The prosecutor of the case turns out to be the female protagonist's sister. The subtext here may be the sister's secret crush on the male protagonist and her internal conflict between doing a good job and being a lenient prosecutor. Because the subtext is generally comprised of the thoughts and feelings that are implied but never stated, it is difficult to write it into the script, but give it a shot. The subplot is often what makes a great story!

Writer Beware!

Practice dividing the films you see into three acts. One good film to view with the three-act structure in mind is **The Conversation**, written and directed by Francis Ford Coppola. Note that the running time is 113 minutes.

The Back Story

The plot and subplot generally rely on the back story—what happens in a plot before the screen story begins. The back story is often conveyed by exposition, or nondialogue text. Although it's important to set the back story elements, many writers tend to over-explain. One way to avoid exposition is by writing flashback scenes that show, rather than explain, what has actually happened in the past, but many producers hate this technique especially when it is used by the novice writer. Too often it is misused because of an inability to write good exposition.

Time Can Play Tricks on You

Consider that you are in the cinema, or watching a videotape at home, and on the screen you see a woman park, get out of her car, and go into a store. Then the film cuts to show the woman taking some milk from the shelves, then it cuts again and she is unlocking her car and putting a brown paper bag on the front seat. You presume, of course, that the brown bag has the milk in it.

That whole but little sequence is in film time, not real time. Had the scene been shot in real time, you would probably have been getting antsy, and thinking, "This is taking forever." Shot in real time, you would have seen the woman go into the store, take a basket and look around; maybe she looked at a lot of shelves and eventually came to the milk section. Perhaps she checked the expiration date on the milk containers before she picked one. Then she went up to the checkout counter. She paid for the milk and had to wait while the cashier took time getting her change. The woman didn't seem to mind the delay. Nothing was said, but she smiled at the cashier and the cashier smiled back. Film time and sequencing allow the audience to see important things, the actions and encounters that add to the story. Understanding film time vs. real time can help make a decent screenwriter become a pro!

Writer Beware!

Don't bother inserting ROLL CREDITS and END CREDITS into your spec script. At the time you submit your spec script, you generally don't know who else is going to be involved in the picture and you won't have any say in the matter anyway.

Looks *Are* Everything

The way that a script looks is very important. Just think, you want to make a good impression, especially if your name is not known by those who will read your script. One important detail is that the script must be written in Courier 12-point or Courier New 12-point. This is equivalent to a typewriter font of 12-point pica. (Believe it or not, some people don't use computers.) Whatever you do, keep away from what you may think are clever, fancy ploys designed to get the reader's attention, like funny colors, illustrations, odd-looking fonts, and the like. Keep it clear and simple!

The reason for using the typewriter font is that the "one page equals one minute of screen time" rule was originally calculated on the typewriter font. To make scripts uniform and therefore to make directors happy, take the time to make this simple change and it can do a world of difference.

It's All in the Details

Scripts should always be three-hole punched and held together with round-headed brass fasteners, often called brads. Just be sure that the fasteners you use are strong; you don't want your hard work falling apart in someone's office! For some reason, it's fashionable to leave the center hole empty. The binding is the reason for the measurement of the left-hand margin—1.5 inches. The right margin should be set at 1 inch and left unjustified (ragged).

Page numbers should appear flush upper right, ½ inch from the top of the page with a double space immediately after. It's a common practice not to number page 1 (this is the same as in a manuscript of a novel).

Hit Trick

You don't necessarily have to follow the three-act format strictly. But it would be better to stick to it in the beginning and wait until you are experienced before you start experimenting. The three-act format is what film people expect; if you don't give it to them, many will be thrown off-kilter.

The Title Page

In the back of this book, in Appendix C, you will find an example of a title page for a spec script. Note that this sample title page includes a note that the script is registered with the WGAw (Writers Guild of America, West). Registering your script with either the guild or the United States Copyright Office is covered in this book. On the line below that one you should type a copyright line.

The cover of your script should be sixty-pound card stock, preferably in black. Put nothing on it at all. When the agents or producers or studios receive it, they will write the name of the screenplay along the spine in marker pen; don't do it yourself. Always use 8.5" × 11" white paper for the script pages.

Also on the title page in the lower right-hand corner, about three inches up from the bottom, you should include your address, phone, fax, and e-mail details. If you happen to have an agent, you would write in his or her name and address and leave your personal stuff out. Don't forget, all the type is in Courier New. (And that's the last reminder!)

Help! Software

Whatever we may think about the computer, it is an established part of all businesses, including the film business.

If you are well educated in the computer world, you could design a template layout for your word-processing program that uses key codes like ALT–S to shift formats from slug-line to character cue and so forth. Otherwise, your options are to do formatting manually, relying on cutting and pasting, or to familiarize yourself with a screenwriting program. If you're confused, don't panic, keep on reading.

Software Programs

A software program designed for screenwriting will make your job much easier. If you are seriously planning to write, it may be well worth the expense. It'll help you keep track of all the material, give you various searching options, minimize the busywork of retyping the character cues and other repeating tags, and save all your revisions, so that you can choose to "undo" the changes at any time.

As with all software programs, the promotional material that comes with screenwriting software programs will tell you how easy life is going to be once you have loaded their goodies. But don't be fooled: You still have to do more than breathe on the screen for your screenplay software to start producing. There is going to be a learning curve, as with anything else, but once you have it down, and it's not that hard, it will cut your writing time down significantly. Below, you will find the top five best-selling software titles as of 2006.

- Final Draft 7 Professional Scriptwriting Win/Mac: $187.99
- Write Brothers Movie Magic Screenwriter (PC & Mac): $159.99
- Hollywood Screenwriter: $29.99
- Final Draft 7/Syd Field's Screenwriting Workshop DVD Bundle: $199.99
- Syd Field's Screenwriting Workshop: $35.99

Luckily, many software companies now offer trial versions that you can download and use for a short while. This way, you can familiarize yourself with the program and what it will allow you to do—as well as how difficult it will be to use—before you make the commitment to purchase it.

Whatever way you decide to go, never forget that what is going to impress people in the long run is the content that you write. Try and follow all the advice about presentation because it's essential, but once you are over that hurdle it's what's in the package that counts.

Chapter 5

Go Ahead, Make a Scene!

Map It Out

The scene is the basic building block of the script. In executing a script, the screenwriter has only a few tools with which to work. These are: locales (choosing the picture), narrative (describing what is taking place in the picture), and dialogue (what is being said in the picture). Together these tools combine and create the building block of the script, "the scene."

The half-hour sitcom, one-hour show, and TV movies use different formats, which will we discuss later, but the same tools apply to all formats. Let's begin with locales.

The locale is a place. It is the picture you use to tell your story. Since it is a place, it has an interior or exterior. In film and television it also has a time. The time is either day or night.

Good scriptwriters use interesting locales. They bring the very best visuals they can to a script because they understand the rule of film—that is, the viewer would rather watch than listen. Remember, what an audience wants to see are pictures. If they only wanted words, they'd buy novels.

Imagine yourself sitting in front of the TV set. Let's say you are watching the successful one-hour show *West Wing*. One of the main characters, Josh, has discovered crucial news that must reach President Bartlett. He has left his office and is moving quickly down the hall.

Others characters join him; they talk while moving. The picture is being seen, or shot, from many angles to get the feeling of action. What you are watching is the work of the director. The director is responsible for the various angles or shots within a given location.

When Josh, however, exits his office, when he enters the hall, and when he finally enters Bartlett's office, you are watching the vision of the scriptwriter. There are three locales in this example: Josh's office, the hallway, and President Bartlett's oval office. The scriptwriter creates the locale; the director decides how to shoot it.

Creating the Visuals

Count how often locales change in a given movie or one-hour episode and you will understand the medium of "moving" pictures. Choosing locales is my favorite part of scripting, especially in the one-hour, TV movie, and feature film. Each picture becomes your canvas, and the pictures you use can change the entire feeling of the show.

Locales do much more than present a picture; they can literally create a mood. Let's suppose you are crafting a scene in which a man for the first time proposes to a woman. You decide the locale should be a steel mill and he is yelling over the grinding industrial noise.

Take the above dialogue, the same two lovers, and place them now on the beach in Malibu. The locale is tranquil; a wave rolls up as they pass. What you will have are two very different scenes, two very different moods.

Writing Locales

At the moment, I am inside my favorite bookstore having a latté. If I were to set up this locale it would look like this:

INT. BOOKSTORE COFFEESHOP — DAY

INT. is interior, the locale is the bookstore coffee shop, and it is day. Now, if I were to step outside and walk to my car would this locale change? Yes, the locale would now be:

EXT. PARKING LOT — DAY

Let's set up the locale you are sitting in right now. Are you in your office? In a special room? Perhaps you are reading this lesson while in some exotic location on vacation. Are you inside, or out? Is it day, or night? Now envision yourself getting up and going someplace else, let's say another room. This, of course would be a new locale.

The Importance of Narrative

Narrative is description. It describes what is taking place in the locale. To generate interest a script must first be a good read, one in which the reader is compelled to turn the page. A good read is a visual read, one in which the movie or TV episode visually plays in the reader's head.

Good narrative is what makes the picture come alive. If we equate choosing the locale to choosing the canvas, then we can equate writing the narrative with filling the canvas in with a paintbrush. Every word in the narrative, every stroke, matters.

A good painter knows when to stop painting the canvas. They know where to leave spaces. Again, less is more. Some locales require more narrative than others. For example, if you are describing a foreign environment such as Tamarindo, Costa Rica, more words will be required than when describing a used car lot in LA. Most of us have not been to Tamarindo, but we are all familiar with what major cities and used parking lots look like. The only narrative needed here would be the price range of the used cars. It could be a lot filled with

Jaguars and Mercedes, or 1989 pick-ups. Other than that nothing more is needed.

But again, lean is the name of the game. Words should be kept to a bare minimum. They should suggest the picture without getting too detailed or tedious.

In *The Harder They Fall*, a comedy Movie of the Week that I scripted, I needed to establish the wrestling area of my protagonist, the "bad boy" of pro-wrestling, Maximus Man. So this is how I wrote it:

```
INT. CONVENTION CENTER - DAY

A packed auditorium of wrestle-maniacs jeer and scream as they
watch MAXIMUM PAYNE, black and white paint on his face, smash a
chair over TENNESSEE TORNADO's head. Resounding "BOOS" come from
the audience.

INT. RING — DAY

Max is tossed off the hip of the giant "DESTROYER." In spite
of his 30-year-old lean, and buffed, six foot frame, he seems
dwarfed in comparison to his opponent.
The crowd goes berserk as Max is slammed down, especially the
women and kids wearing "I Love Max" T-shirts. They yell from the
front row "Rearrange his face, Max, it can't get any uglier!"

INT. STANDING OUTSIDE THE RING - DAY

Is QUEEN MARY the Destroyer's infamous female manager, decked in
black, wearing a crown, and with a monkey, KONG, perched on her
shoulder. She screams profanities at Max.

INT. RING - DAY

Max disentangles himself from the ropes, charges back, scores
with a knee to the head, body drops the Destroyer. The crowd
roars its approval of the gnarly glitz -- the forces of good and
evil clearly defined in one of the last arenas where the good
guys win.
```

The Challenge

Writing good narrative is a challenge. The writer must always ask, what are the words that most descriptively or metaphorically get my message across? The wonderful thing about writers is that no two writers will ever choose the same thing.

Narrative tells a story. In the original *Rocky*, Rocky Balboa comes off a streetcar somewhere in Philly. He sees a derelict on the street and pulls him under an awning. When he returns home we discover home is a beat up apartment with an old mattress hanging up for a punching bag.

He takes down his pet fish, Moby Dick, and puts him next to his pet turtle, so they can keep each other company. Now he walks to the mirror, looks at his trashed face, which has been beaten up sparring in the ring. He looks at a hanging picture of himself as a young boy and then looks back in the mirror at what he has become. He grabs ice from the refrigerator, plops it on his head, and then collapses on the bed. From this moment on we love him. We root for him. We would even get in the ring with him.

The above narrative tells us about Rocky without dialogue. It is all done visually through the narrative. As you can see, narrative also reveals character. A novelist can reveal the inner monologue or the thoughts of the character's head; this is not so for the scriptwriter.

Writer Beware!

"Writing energy is like anything else. The more you put in, the more you get out."— Richard Reeves, an American writer, syndicated columnist, and lecturer.

On film, the only thing that can indicate what a character is thinking is by what they do or say. Let's say the character is a billionaire. He drives up to a posh restaurant in his new Jaguar. As the valet takes his car he notices a dollar bill dropped on the ground. When no one is looking he picks it up and sticks it in his pocket.

What do we know about this character? Actions speak louder than words. This is a man who, when he opens the menu will scan the prices first. So who is he? Obviously an eccentric, but a man who had to struggle for everything he has. Is he a CEO about to go down with the company? Whatever his story, he's interesting, and we the audience are caught up in the discovery process.

Each basic scene should perform the following:

- Move the story forward.
- Move the main character closer to or further away from his or her goal.
- Add to the viewers' understanding of the character.
- Be a logical and necessary part of the story.
- Show how the characters involved feel.
- Be compelling—contain either conflict or the foreshadowing of it, or show an unexpected alliance between opponents.
- Keep viewers eager to learn what happens next.

Once you've got a basic outline of your scenes, you'll have to pick the first one to start working on. It doesn't necessarily have to be the first scene, which is arguably the most important scene of the screenplay. Whatever you find that works for you, do it. In fact, you can start out small, writing small connecting scenes that would appear later in the film.

The First Scene

One of your most important objectives is now going to be the drafting of the first ten pages—"the deadly ten." Not to scare you, but these pages can make or break your chances of making a movie.

Roughly, this is what happens when a reader picks up your spec script. First of all, the reader gauges the overall appearance of the script, maybe flipping over a few pages to establish that the writer knows how to format a spec script. If all that looks as if the writer knows what he or she is up to, then it's directly to the first page, which should begin with FADE IN.

Writer Beware!

If in doubt, cut it out. Learn to trust your intuition; if you get a gut feeling that something isn't working for some reason, you don't have to fret endlessly over it—get rid of it and see whether what you've written plays better with the cut. Invariably, the piece will be improved.

Let's say your script has passed stage one. Now the reader wants to find out what the story is about. The reader's eyes scan the opening scene. Remember, you have only ten minutes—ten pages— to grab and hold the reader; otherwise, your script is moved to the rejection pile.

Ask yourself: What are you going to include in your first ten pages?

Storyboarding vs. Stepping Out Scenes

Many directors "storyboard" their scripts, even if they can hardly draw. Hitchcock was, perhaps, the most famous director who storyboarded his scripts. In fact, he went so far as to say that the actual shooting was boring because he had already shot the film in his head.

What is storyboarding? It's the process of producing sketches of the shots of your script. This is the director's job. The writer's job is stepping out the scenes. Nothing ticks off a director more than a writer telling him how to shoot his movie. It is enough that you create the pictures; let the director decide how to shoot them.

Hit Trick

Try to get a copy of **Rear Window**, directed by Alfred Hitchcock. Pay attention to how one scene flows into the next. Remember, Hitchcock was famous for storyboarding his films.

Laying the Development Groundwork

If a scene does not progress a story forward, if it does not provide new plot information or new revelations of character it belongs in the trash. I was once told by Earl Wallace, writer of the screenplay *Witness* that any time his scenes run over 3½ pages, which equals about 3½ minutes he gets very nervous and cuts them back. Why? Because the audience wants "moving pictures." Since there are so many scenes in a screenplay, it helps me to think of the scenes in units. For example:

> In unit-1, (approximately the first ten pages) the tone is established, the main players, and their world.
> In unit-2, (approximately pages ten to twenty) building conflict and complications propel the story forward.
> In unit-3 (approximately pages twenty to thirty) more complications and conflicts build to the Act-1 plot point.

A plot point is like a miniclimax, it is more than just a story point, it the crucial story point that comes in and totally shifts the action into another direction.

Units: Broken Down

To help us better understand let's continue walking through the first unit, the setup, of a screenplay *The Harder They Fall*. As you recall in the first scene I established Max in his burlesque world of wrestling.

Unit I

In the next scene I established my female lead, Jordan Abernathy, an up and coming attorney, from the world of San Francisco's elite. I also needed to establish the high profile case Jordan is working on. I choose to cut between the chaos of the wrestling arena and courthouse to show that although these two unlikely types live in different worlds their work arenas are both outrageous.

EXT. SAN FRANCISCO FEDERAL COURTHOUSE - DAY

Angry picketers CHANT "MAKE HIM PAY, MAKE HIM PAY!" The doors
bolt open. Flashes go off. Voracious press and television media
surge forward. It's a total fiasco like the scene at the Convention Center, only here the maniacs are the media and the squared
ring our legal system.

Federal Prosecutor FRANK SHAW and his team of attorneys emerge.
Prominent among them is JORDAN ABERNATHY. Beneath Armani wire-
rims is a knockout of a woman in her late 20s.

Standing next to her is friend and co-worker, PATTY PIZZO, not
as pretty, and constantly battling the bulge. Jordan eyes Shaw,
speaks to Patti under her breath.

                    JORDAN
          And once again he avoids the cameras.
          Shaw heads straight for the mini-cams.

                    PATTY
          He's got book deal written all over him.

                    REPORTER #1
          I'm here with Federal Prosecutor, Frank
          Shaw, and his team of attorneys. . . .
          Will Bechman walk?

                    SHAW
          Bechman has perpetrated one of the
          largest corporate frauds in American his-
          tory. He's left families destitute and
          the elderly penniless. We will prove his
          guilt. You have my word on it.

Jordan and Patty pass enraged employees holding Signs: "BECHMAN'S
A THIEF," "HE STOLE MY 401K."

CEO PETER BECHMAN and Defense Attorney BAYLOR HASTINGS, surrounded by press: "What about the wire fraud charges?" "Prosecution's charging money laundering and racketeering."

                         HASTINGS
              CEO Peter Bechman is innocent on all
              charges. My client had no knowledge of the
              accounting practices and blatant crimi-
              nality of his financial officers at Bec-
              worth International.

                          PATTY
              Sure slick. And I wear a size 2.

INT. CONVENTION CORRIDOR - DAY

Max is signing autographs and roughhousing with the young boys
we saw in the front row. He clearly eats it up.

                         BOY#1
              You're awesome Maximus. Tornado ate it
              with that skitz spinecrusher.

                         Boy #2
              Without Boz and Killer you could have
              wasted him.

                          Max
              Next time I'll squash them all like
              cockroaches.

INT. CONVENTION LOCKER ROOM - SAME TIME

CLOSE ON A NEEDLEPOINT

Huge fingers carefully pull the thread. The detail is master-
fully worked; it's Van Gogh's "The Sunflowers."

CAMERA GOES BIGGER, the giant Destroyer is doing the needlepoint. Killer Whale is standing in front of the mirror shaving
his flame-tattooed head. Queen Mary's feeding Kong a banana.

                        KILLER
          I'm gonna try waxing.

                        DESTROYER
          It's painful as shit. I almost ripped off
          my six pack.

Tornado's on the cellular.

                        TORNADO
          Your mother's right, hitting doesn't solve
          anything.

Destroyer shows Killer his needlework.

                        DESTROYER
          You like?

                        KILLER
          What is it?

                        DESTROYER
          Van Gogh's "Sunflowers." You think I should
          have gone with Monet's "Lilies"?

                        KILLER
          Can't you needlepoint Nascars or
          something?

                        TORNADO
                     (into phone)
          He did what to you? Then squash him like a
          turd and smash his face in! Put your mom
          back on.

Reggie is off in the corner, going over some numbers with Boz.

                        REGGIE
          Say you invest 30 grand . . . over a
          twenty year period you can make 80 grand on
          your investment.

> BOZ
> 30 grand is a lot of money.

> MARY
> Boz, how long can you fall on your head?
> You need an IRA.

> BOZ
> How do I know I can trust him?

> REGGIE
> Who?

> BOZ
> Ira. In twenty years what if he doesn't
> remember me? He could get Alzheimers, or
> something.

Queen Mary and Reggie exchange looks.

Max comes in, the boys trailing behind.

> MAX
> Reg, give the kids something.

Reggie opens the closet. A WOMAN jumps out and throws herself at Max.

> WOMAN
> You're rotten, Max. Give it to me hard. I
> don't deserve any better.

The boys eyes go wide.

> MAX
> How about a T-shirt?

Unit 2

The second unit of the setup is a series of scenes in which I reveal more of Jordan's life—that she is alone and wanting a relationship, that she is idealistic when it comes to romance, and that her pragmatist friend, Patti, is always trying to get her to settle for less, out of the fear of not finding anyone. It is also established that Jordan is at the bottom of the totem pole in her firm, and her terrible egomaniac boss intends to keep her there.

```
EXT. SAN FRANCISCO - NOB HILL - NIGHT

NORMAN, attractive, but self-consumed, escorts Jordan from a
posh restaurant. The valet brings up his Porsche.

INT. MOVING WITH PORSCHE - NIGHT

                         NORMAN
             We got the best table in the house. It's
             all about power.

For Jordan it's all about getting home.

INT. PARK MARINA TOWNHOUSES - NIGHT

Norman walks Jordan to the door, takes her keys.

                         JORDAN
             Thank you, Norman. . . .

                         NORMAN
             The honors banquet for my firm is on the
             22nd. Be my date.

She responds by taking back her keys. Undaunted Norman leans
against the door.

                         NORMAN
             I'm featured in "San Francisco Focus" and
             you've got the media on the Bechman trial.
             It's good to be seen together.

                         JORDAN
             I'd rather get audited.

And with that she shuts the door in his face.
```

INT. JORDAN'S APARTMENT

Jordan comes in, takes off her coat, and punches the button on her answering machine.
As the messages play, she crosses to a bird cage that houses a cockatiel by the name of JAKE.

> MACHINE
> Jordan, it's Patty. Jeff's been seeing someone else the whole time we've been dating!

> JORDAN
> What a jerk.

Jake mimics her.

> JAKE
> Jerk. Jerk.

> MACHINE
> What a jerk. . . .Should I not let on that I know? It's hard to find a man who is your professional equal.

INT. SAN FRANCISCO FEDERAL BUILDING - THE NEXT DAY

Jordan and Patty walk through the busy outer offices.

> PATTY
> Maybe it'll blow over. . . . If I pretend I don't know, then it won't look bad if I don't do anything.

> JORDAN
> Patty, would you listen to yourself?

> PATTY
> So I'm desperate! Are you going out with Norman again?

> JORDAN
> In my nightmares.

                    PATTY
     The qualities you're searching for in a
     man do not exist in the male species.

                    JORDAN
     I think they do.

                    PATTY
     And what brought you to that conclusion?

                    JORDAN
     The study of Chimps. I minored in
     anthropology.

                    PATTY
     Maybe you didn't see the sequel, but Kong's
     dead.

Jordan rolls her eyes.

                    PATTY (cont'd)
     Celibacy shortens your life span. They're
     also tracing it now to make pattern bald-
     ness in women. It's dangerous being
     picky. You could die young and check out
     hairless.

EXT. SEATTLE CONVENTION CENTER - DAY

The parking lot is full.

INT. UNDERGROUND CORRIDOR

No one is around. We can hear the noise of the fans from above.
Reggie is nervously pacing, talking on the phone.

                    REGGIE
     This is important! I need to talk to him
     now.

A PHONE TAP - LOCATION UNKNOWN
The conversation being recorded.

```
INT. SAN FRANCISCO FEDERAL BUILDING - OUTER OFFICES

                         RECEPTIONIST
              (on phone)
              Sir, I told you, Mr. Shaw is not available,
              he's in a meeting. I can let you talk to
              one of his associates.

INT. JORDAN'S OFFICE

The PHONE RINGS.  Jordan picks.

                         JORDAN
              Abernathy . . . Hello?

No response.

                      INTERCUT/REGGIE
              He hesitates.

                         JORDAN
              Who is this?
```

In unit 2, the phone call leads Jordan to the Seattle Convention center during a wrestling match. While secretly meeting with Reggie two men come in and kill him. Max comes on the scene and gets her out of the way.

Unit 3

In the last unit of action leading to the plot point they discover they have been set up and the two of them, who from the get-go cannot stand one another, end up on the lamb together.

```
INT. PATTY'S OFFICE - FOLLOWING

                         JORDAN
              Cover for me, Patty.  I can be back in five
              hours.
```

                              PATTY
          Are you out of your mind!? We could both
          lose our jobs for this.

                              JORDAN
          It's Callahan! I can feel it. This is the
          physical evidence we've been looking for.

                              PATTY
          He disappears before the company's col-
          lapse and for two years nobody can find
          him. Now he calls from Seattle and offers
          you a key to a safety deposit box?

                              JORDAN
          He says he has a signed memo from Bechman
          ordering him to lie about the stocks.

                              PATTY
          What if it's a hoax?

                              JORDAN
          Shaw never has to know.

                              PATTY
          Jordan, I have a very bad feeling about
          this. That astrologer I went to said I'm
          having a Saturn return.

Jordan leaves. Patty calls after her.

                         PATTY (cont'd)
          I'm on shaky ground already. My life could
          come crashing down at any moment.

The phone rings; Patty freezes.

                         PATTY (cont'd)
          Oh, God!

She cautiously picks up the receiver.

                    PATTY (cont'd)
      . . . Pizzo.
                    SHAW (O.S.)
      Tell Abernathy I want the two of you in my
      conference room at 6:00.

                    PATTY (cont'd)
      Yes, Sir. (hangs up, then yells) Whose got
      the want ads?

She quickly goes to Google and types in "Greg's List."

EXT. SAN FRANCISCO INTERNATIONAL AIRPORT - DAY
Jordan shows her ticket, boards the gate.

A MAN ON A CELLULAR
Watching her.

                    THE MAN
            She's on. Don't let her out of your
            sight.

EXT. SEATTLE CONVENTION CENTER - DAY

A black four-by is waiting near the parking entrance.

INT. FOUR-BY

The man behind the wheel is a lethal-looking Chinese-American named
SU LEE. Next to him is HARRY PENCHUK, an aging linebacker gone soft.

                    PENCHUK
            You know how much they pocket in a night?
            Around 600 grand. I saw it on A&E.

Jordan pulls up in a rented car, pays at the gate. Lee spots her,
grabs the cellular.

                    LEE
            We got her.

> VOICE OVER THE CELL
> Don't call back until you have the key.

INT. SEATTLE CONVENTION CENTER - DAY

It's wall to wall screaming fans. Jordan looks about as comfortable as Martha Stewart at the MTV Awards. On stage is an empty 3,000 pound steel cage with 15-foot bars.

> ANNOUNCER (OVER PA)
> . . . It's the moment we've been waiting for -- the SuperSlam event of the evening, the "Battle Royale!" with four of the hottest superstars in the ring today!

The audience goes ballistic.

> ANNOUNCER (cont'd)
> . . . The mighty, unsinkable, "Killer Whale."

Killer comes out, clenches his fists, and convulses his tattooed head.

> ANNOUNCER (cont'd)
> . . . SuperSlams's one-man demolition . . . the "Destroyer!"

Queen Mary grabs his ammo belt, plants a big wet one on his lips. A bow-tied referee has to pry her away.

> ANNOUNCER (cont'd)
> . . . Winner of the prized Intercontinental title, "Tennessee Tornado!"

"Tornado" roars into the cage like a twister in a coonskin cap.

> ANNOUNCER (cont'd)
> . . . The mean and vicious inflictor of pain . . . pain of the worst intensity . . . "Maximum Payne!"

Max comes out to BOOS and HISSES and threatens the audience. Somebody in the front row annoys him. He goes for the rope. The Ref pulls him back. Max drop-kicks him and lays him flat.

Jordan does a double take. "BOOS" flood the auditorium.

INT. FEDERAL BUILDING - SHAW'S OFFICE - EVENING

A very nervous Patty takes a seat with the rest of the tired team. Jordan is conspicuously missing.

>   SHAW
>   Where's Abernathy?

>   PATTY
>   She's not feeling so well, Sir. She had
>   to leave.

>   SHAW
>   Why wasn't I informed?

All wait on her response.

>   PATTY
>   She was afraid to come in contact with
>   anybody. It's bad, Sir . . .   aching
>   muscles . . . a high fever. . . . It
>   sounds like that Avian thing. Maybe we
>   should stock up on Tamaflu. She could
>   be the mutated cross-over.

INT. SEATTLE CONVENTION CENTER - EVENING

Jordan checks her watch. It's not quite time yet.

In the STEEL CAGE the four wrestlers face off. Max bodyslams the Destroyer, hurls him into Tornado, who's got Killer in an airplane spin. Four mounds of flesh collapse.

Lee has his eye on Jordan, but Penchuk is so into the massacre, Lee has to pull him away.

INT. UNDERGROUND DESERTED HALLWAY

Jordan finds Reggie nervously waiting for her.

> JORDAN
>
> Mr. Callahan?

> REGGIE
>
> Where's Shaw?

> JORDAN
>
> I can take you to him.
> I'm his associate.

She shows her ID.

> REGGIE
>
> You told me you were bringing Shaw.

> JORDAN
>
> We're Federal prosecutors. I can grant you
> immunity and give you protection. But I
> need the memo.

> REGGIE
>
> It's in a safety deposit box.

> JORDAN
>
> Where?

Reggie reluctantly removes a key from his pocket.

> REGGIE
>
> Merchant's Bank in San Francisco.

> JORDAN
>
> We'll go there together. Let's get you on
> the first plane out of here.

Max, just off the stage, COMES AROUND THE CORNER.

> MAX
>
> Hey, Reg, I've been trying to. . . .

He SPOTS Lee and Penchuk come into the corridor, silencers in hand.

>   MAX (cont'd)
>   Look out!

Reggie and Jordan turn. Lee and Penchuk FIRE. . . . Max shoves them out of the way. The three bolt around the corner -- and come racing down the corridor. More SHOTS. This time Reggie is hit. The key drops from his hand. Jordan grabs it. Max pushes her into a weight room, manages to pull Reggie in after them.

INT. WEIGHT ROOM

He grabs a set of barbells, wedges them against the door and drops to Reggie's side. Max rips open his blood-stained shirt.

>   MAX
>   Reg . . . it's a lethal wound to the
>   chest.

>   MAX (cont'd)
>   Reggie. . . .

Max feels for a pulse. He's overwrought and can barely get the words out.

>   MAX (cont'd)
>   . . . He's dead.

The men start hammering on the door.

EXT. CORRIDOR
They hear someone coming, stash their guns.

It's a ghoulish looking wrestler. Dental tools are hanging from his belt.

INT. WEIGHT ROOM - SAME TIME

Max grabs a hand weight, shatters a street-level vent window, helps Jordan through, manages to squeeze himself out.

INT. CORRIDOR

The wrestler drops a drill. Penchuk picks it up.

>   PENCHUK (in awe)
>   You're Doctor Death.

He hands him the drill. "Death" buzzes it in Penchuk's face.

EXT. PARKING LOT - NIGHT

Max and Jordan reach a motorcycle in a heavy downpour. He pulls a spare key from a magnetized box underneath.

>   MAX
>   Get on!

He cranks it.

>   JORDAN
>   That?

>   MAX
>   Or stay here, lady. It's up to you.

Jordan quickly straddles the seat.

EXT. CONVENTION CENTER

Lee and Penchuk come rushing out, spot Max and Jordan as they take off.

MOVING WITH MAX'S BIKE
Jordan, holds on for dear life. They hit a mud puddle. It sprays all over them. Jordan loses her bag.

>   JORDAN
>   Hey, that's my Prada!

EXT. POLICE STATION - DOWNTOWN SEATTLE - NIGHT

The bike comes to a screeching halt in front of the station. The body paint covering Max's bare chest and face has all run together. Jordan gets off, covered in mud and paint.

                    JORDAN (cont'd)
          It's a shame there weren't some barrels
          back there, you could have jumped them!

                    MAX
          We weren't wearing helmets.

INT. POLICE STATION

A tired, disgruntled detective, AL SANCHEZ, sits behind his messy desk, a phone to his ear, Max and Jordan facing him. He's about had it with the bizarre looking duo.

He hangs up.

                    SANCHEZ
          What's the joke?

                    JORDAN
          Joke?

                    SANCHEZ
          There's no body where you said there was
          a body. Nobody heard anything. Nobody saw
          anything.

                    MAX
          I saw my manager, Reggie Tucker, get
          killed!

                    JORDAN
          His name is Callahan.

                    SANCHEZ
          It doesn't matter what they call him.
          There's no body.
     (suspiciously, to Jordan)
          You're a Fed?

                    JORDAN
    I'm an Assistant Federal Attorney, working
    on the Bechman case.

                    SANCHEZ
    Where's your ID?

                    JORDAN
    In my bag which I lost.
    (shoots Max a dirty look)
    Call my boss, Federal Prosecutor, Frank
    Shaw. He'll vouch for me.

                    SANCHEZ
    What's his cell number?

Now, he's got her.

INT. CORRIDOR

Sanchez tosses Max and Jordan out, slamming the door behind
them. They move down the corridor.

                    JORDAN
    If you didn't drive like Evel Knievel I
    would have had my Blackberry.

                    MAX
    Those guys who were riding our ass, what
    did they want?

                    JORDAN
    (with sarcasm)
    There's a strong likelihood it was your
    manager. And we can identify them.
    (then)
    How much money do you have on you?

                    MAX
    (holds out his shorts)
    I have one pocket, lady. If it doesn't
    bother you, I'll show you what's in it.

INT. PATTY'S CONDO - NIGHT

Patty, in sweats, and wearing a facial mask, is on the tread. The phone rings. She picks up the remote.

INTERCUT:

Jordan at a police pay phone

                         JORDAN
          Patty?

                         PATTY
          Where are you? Do you have Callahan?

                         JORDAN
          He was murdered. Two men shot him in front
          of me.

Patty freezes, the belt keeps moving. She almost falls on her face.

                         JORDAN (cont'd)
          Patty, are you there?

                         PATTY
          . . . Yeah, yeah . . . I'm here.

                         JORDAN
          I'm at a Seattle police station. Can you
          wire me some money?

Max spots something, clamps a hand over Jordan's mouth, drags her behind a corner. Her eyes open wide.

                    PATTY (OVER RECEIVER)
          Jordan? . . . Talk to me!

Penchuk and Lee approach the desk sergeant. The men flash police badges.

> LEE
> Lee and Penchuk. San Francisco PD. We're
> looking for a woman named Abernathy. She's
> traveling with a wrestler. . . .

> SERGEANT
> Yeah, Max Payne, I got his autograph.
> They're with Detective Sanchez. Last door
> on the left.

The men head down the hall.

> SERGEANT (cont'd)
> What are they wanted for?

> PENCHUK
> Murder.

Max and Jordan exchange incredulous looks. They hightail it out of there, leaving Patty on the line.

> PATTY (OS)
> . . . Jordan!? Grunt, give me some sign
> of life. . . .

EXT. POLICE STATION - NIGHT

They hop on the motorcycle, glance back, see Lee and Penchuk coming out. Max burns rubber.[ENDEXT]

Chapter 6

Reel People: Characters

The Main Attraction: Your Protagonist

Structure holds the story in place, but it is character, scene by scene, line by line, that takes you through the script.

Once you have determined the spine, time frame, and turning points of the story you are writing, your characters are next. If fully developed, they will tell you where to go next. The characters will be the ones moving the story forward. If they are not properly developed your characters will be automatons stuck inside a plot connecting the dots.

I had been successful in television for a number of years when a producer, the late Phil Mandelker, called my partner and me in for our first assignment with a Movie of the Week. We were thrilled. When we got to the studio Phil told us the spine of what he wanted. It was essentially a soap, a story about two women in a love-hate relationship who grew up together as friends.

At the top of the movie one of the women is very successful, the other is desperately trying to keep afloat. They meet again as adult women and their lives once again become entwined, this time with the same man.

We bounced ideas around with Phil and were told to go home and develop the characters. He said to develop the main protagonist, Sharon, and to call him up when we were ready.

Having had experience only in episodic television, where characters for the most part are already established, we jotted down a few quick pages and brought them back to Phil. I will never forget sitting in his office watching him read those pages. After a few moments, he looked at me and asked, "Do you call this writing?"

Instead of cutting us off (writers' jargon for getting axed), Phil worked with us for the next two weeks helping us develop our characters. I consider this experience as one of the high points of my career. What he taught me I teach in my classes today. I have yet to find a character development process that works better.

Writing Characters

We began with the characters' history, or back life—that is, everything of consequence that had taken place in their lives before the film began. Who were their parents? How much money did they have? Where did they live? Did they compete with their brother or sister? Were they popular in school? Did they struggle over grades, or did things come easily to them?

Phil asked "When was their first sexual experience? How were they perceived by the opposite sex? Who were their friends in the neighborhood? What side of the tracks did they live on? What church did they go to?" And on and on it went, to the point I thought of being absurd.

Writer Beware!

Forrest Gump was the epitome of an original, unique character. There was certainly no one else in the picture remotely like him. The character was based on the one in Winston Groom's novel of the same name. It was an excellent example of consistency of characterization. The screenplay was by Eric Roth.

At the time I thought this kind of minutia was ridiculous, there was no way in hell we were going to get this into the script.

I failed to see how knowing how much money my Sharon's parents had in the bank or when she was born would have any effect on our two-hour movie. But I went along with it regardless. After all, he was the producer and we were the writers, and I wasn't stupid. If nothing else came out of this, at least we were making a good contact.

But a very odd thing happened. After a few of these sessions I found myself getting totally caught up in them. I found myself thinking about Sharon a lot. On my long one-hour commute to and from Phil's house, I'd wonder how Sharon would react and relate to other characters in the script. How she dressed. What was in her desk drawers? Her apartment and how it was decorated. What her day timer looked like and more.

I even wondered how she would relate to people in my own life! It was as though she was beginning to exist on some invisible plane. She was alive. I thought about her like you do a real person. It was as though the clay had breath.

Our protagonist, Sharon, was a high-powered female executive. One day Phil asked me, "What does her office look like?" I said, "It's exquisite!" He bellowed, "What the hell is exquisite?" I jumped, completely intimidated. Suddenly, I was being made to think like a filmmaker! He was forcing me to think visually.

The office no longer was just exquisite. It became marble and muted pastels, Renoir sketches, a Louis XIV desk, and decor audacious enough to compete with the city skyline. It was eccentric and exceedingly feminine, like the president who occupied it.

To this day, Sharon, in *California Reunion*, is one of my favorite characters. I came to know her like you would an intimate friend. I could write pages on her years growing up. I knew her favorite color. I knew the defining moments in her history that made a permanent impact on her life, such things as:

- Her abusive father and the alcoholic mother who had resigned herself to living with him.
- The humiliation her parents had caused her in school.
- Her early sexual permissiveness and the skeletons in her closet.
- Her climb to the top of the corporate ladder. She was talented but she also used her assets to manipulate men.

Suddenly pictures started coming into my mind. The pictures became locales. The people in Sharon's life started popping up and they become the characters in my movie! I was not conscious of it then, but I was doing much more than just character development, I was developing the entire movie!

Remember this; keep it at the forefront of your mind: When developing the character's back story don't concern yourself with how you can put it in the script. You're jumping ahead and looking in the wrong place. Don't make assumptions that the rewards of such background work will come to you as you write the script. Stay with it!

It is amazing, but through investigating your main character, other characters will happen, locales will be created, and dialogue will come to life. It is as though these characters are helping you to develop your script. They are not automatons in the plot, they actually start talking to you, directing your way, telling you where they go, the places they frequent, who and what they value.

The Character's Present Life

With the back life complete, focus turns to the present life of the characters. The present includes everything of significance in their professional, personal, and private lives once the film begins.

Professional: How the characters relate and interact at work.
Personal: How the characters relate and interact with family and friends.
Private: What the characters do when no one is watching.

The Professional Life of the Character

A character's professional life is more than an office or a title. It is a series of moving pictures, not just one locale. It is a routine. It becomes their alarm clock, what they eat for breakfast, the building they live in, the Starbucks they habitually pull into, the way they order their latté, and the route they drive to work.

Writer Beware!

Rent a copy of **The Odd Couple** (1968). Written by Neil Simon, starring Jack Lemmon and Walter Matthau. Apart from being an absolute hoot, it's a fine example of how the dialogue suits each character and contributes to their diametrically opposed lives.

When your character arrives at the office, is there a space reserved for him in a subterranean parking lot? Is there a doorman who greets him? On what floor is their office? When he gets off the elevator, how wide is the hallway? When he reaches the office, what does the doorman say? Inside, how many secretaries are at work? How many phones are ringing? What do the pictures on the walls reveal? Who is your character's secretary? What is their relationship? Is it business? Are they the best of friends, or is it more intimate? Who are his partners and the people he works with? Remember, these people are the possible characters in your script. Who comes in, who goes out? See it in your head.

The Personal Life of the Character

This aspect of the character's life is everything that is not professional or private. Just think of your own personal life. Who are the people in it? How do you interact socially? What are your hobbies? Where do you frequent? What does your personal world look like?

Let's begin with the family. Is your character married? Who is he/she married to? What is the interaction between the couple? What do they talk about? Is their sex life spontaneous or do they only consider making love on the weekends? We have all been to parties and in social situations where we have seen couples who are outwardly pleasant, caring, and even loving, and yet there is an obvious unspoken tension between them. What about your couple. What are they hiding? What do they show to the world, and what do they show to each other? Identify your characters' relationships and how these relationships change over the course of the story.

In my advanced workshop, I have an exercise where writers must create a sequence of visuals revealing who the character or characters are without having them in one single shot. We can tell who they are by their environment. A character's surroundings will give you great insights.

Hit Trick

"The whole thing is, you've got to make them care about somebody." —Frank Capra, was an Academy Award–winning Italian-American film director. He also helped to create films, including the classics **It's a Wonderful Life** and **Mr. Smith Goes to Washington**.

Into the personal life of the character come friends. Who are they? With whom has your character chosen to associate? What do your characters like to do socially? What sports are they into? Golf? Bowling? Softball? These pictures will become your locales. When you develop your characters' personal lives, you are developing a large portion of your television pilot or movie.

The Private Life of the Character

Private moments are an open window into the soul of your character. A private moment is what your character does when no one is looking. Unfortunately, in most spec scripts I rarely find private moments.

I recently saw *About Schmidt* with Jack Nicholson. Schmidt's character was superbly crafted. He was so layered, so vacant, so deprived of his own potential that you ached for him. You might say it was the brilliance of Jack Nicholson that made the movie, but it was the character of Schmidt that brought the likes and the genius of Jack Nicholson on board to want to play him.

This film was filled with private moments. We watch Schmidt through the difficult ritual of retirement, struggling with a lack of self-esteem, a lack of purpose, and trying to find a reason to get up in the morning. And then we watch him as widower forced to face this new phase of his life alone. We laugh at him, we cry with him, and we dread becoming like him. No matter what our circumstances are in life we identity with this character's futility and humanity.

There were wonderful private moments in *Rocky 1* where we, the audience, saw into the has-been boxer's soul. Early in the film, Rocky enters his run-down apartment where an old mattress serves as a makeshift punching bag. We sense his loneliness. In this private moment our hearts go out to this man.

The Compelling Characteristic

You now have anywhere from five to perhaps fifteen pages on your character. You know his back life and his present life, which you have broken down into professional, personal, and private categories. How can you take this information and translate it to film? For this purpose we turn to the compelling characteristic.

Think about your character. Ask yourself which characteristic is the most dominant or profound. What single trait drives him the most? At first, this process may seem highly simplistic. You may feel that in playing only one compelling characteristic your character may appear one-dimensional.

We have discussed the importance of identifying the spine of the story in previous chapters. This process is also simplistic. It is this very simplicity that enables the writer to stay on track! "A lost alien is befriended by a young boy who helps him find his way back home."

This spine is from *E. T. The Extra Terrestrial.* But it is not all about *E. T.* The story is filled with twists, turns, surprises, jeopardy, suspense, and numerous subplots, but the spine is the cohesive thrust: everything attaches to it. The entire story is inherent in those few words.

The same can be said about the compelling characteristic. The character is multidimensional but there is one dominant force that motivates the character the most. Playing the compelling characteristic keeps us, the audience, rooted in clarity; it defines and keeps the character on track. . . .

The unforgettable Rocky Balboa's compelling characteristic is his compassion. Writer Sylvester Stallone plays it out in almost every scene. Rocky pulls winos off the street, tells hookers to go home, and stops and talks to orphaned animals in pet shops.

Employed as a strong arm for a numbers runner, Rocky gives the client another chance. He finds a very plain woman beautiful, and he doesn't even dislike his adversary, Apollo Creed. Who wouldn't be rooting for this character? We care so much for him that in the last ten minutes of the film we're inside the ring taking our licks with him!

Writers often ask me how much character work is necessary for secondary and minor cast members. Is this kind of detail needed for them? No. I only do such intense work on my main characters. It was much less for the supporting cast of Felicia and Jerry Weiner, possibly a third of that. Come to know your main characters like you would a member of your family.

I only do such intense work on my main characters. As you do your work on them you will come to know your secondary characters. They will require much less work.

You can use the compelling characteristic even for a bit part or a walk-on. It is a wonderful device and gives the character a point of view and an attitude.

An underdeveloped protagonist results in a one-dimensional script, whereas intense character work, not only opens the screenwriter visually, but also develops other aspects of the script.

The people in your characters' personal and professional lives become characters in your story. Their routines and the places they frequent become your locales. Their compelling characteristic becomes the force that moves the action forward.

There's Got to Be a "Bad Guy"

The antihero isn't exactly a villain. He is a hero who lacks positive qualities that you normally associate with the protagonist. Some hard-boiled protagonists are in fact antiheroes. They are far too cynical to come off as brave, honest, and unselfish, though by the end of the film they'll win the affections of the audience—and perhaps of the female lead as well. Ironically, it's their antihero qualities that endear them to the viewers.

The antihero philosophy is summed up nicely in a line spoken by one of the movies' top antiheros, Rick (played by Humphrey Bogart), in *Casablanca*. It's delivered in reply to Inspector Renault's warning about Ungarte, a character played by Peter Lorre, who is to be arrested in Rick's place for the murder of two German couriers who were carrying the letters of transit. As Rick put it, "I stick my neck out for nobody."

The Chemistry Created

Your protagonist should always move the action forward. How? Through conflict. How is that conflict created? By not giving them what they want. The stronger the dramatic need and the stronger the obstacles, the stronger your protagonist.

Here is the formula:

Strong dramatic need + obstacles = the conflict = action

The harder you make it for your protagonist, the more we root for them. Remember, it is not what you hand them, but how you block them that creates their next move.

Writing Action

For the sake of illustration, let's not deal with pure action films. The reason for this is that they are mostly the armed-conflict type of action without too much in the way of subtlety. What actually constitutes action: conflict, as in the above formula.

Take a simple situation: A registered letter from a debtor threatening legal action arrives at the protagonist's home. The character sits down to read the letter. The room is well lit and tastefully furnished. The man is good-looking and dressed in chinos, topsiders, and an open-necked checked shirt.

The man looks up to the window because he can hear his children playing outside; he registers worry and concern. The door to the room opens and his wife comes in. She is wearing white tennis gear. She's an attractive woman.

The wife is curious to know what's in the letter. The husband passes it to her. She reads it and reacts: "What are we going to do?" The husband doesn't answer; he puts his head in his hands. Thus, a letter starts a chain of events. Even if this were the first scene in the picture, the audience is already gathering valuable information.

They obviously know the family is in financial trouble and that the husband is not at work. Without consciously knowing it, they have also absorbed the social strata of the couple: they live in a very nice home, they have some children who are playing in a garden, they are wearing typical upwardly mobile clothes, and they look good in them. Having taken that in, the audience has added to it their own opinions, which are subject to their experiences as well as their prejudices—the audience brings everything they are to the viewing. It is important that the scriptwriter realizes what is going on in the viewers' minds.

Another Version

Using exactly the same scene plot, let's look at how an audience might react if only a few of the details were changed. A man is sitting in a room reading a letter. The room is cluttered with junk; in one corner there are stacks of unread newspapers. The man is wearing old jeans and a workingman's shirt; he needs a shave. The man looks up to the window and grimaces at the loud noise some children are making; he takes out a cigarette and lights it.

The door opens and a woman comes in. She is wearing an old dress with an apron tied around her waist. Her hair is long and unkempt. She looks at the letter. "You got another of them damn things?" The man doesn't look up. He drags on his cigarette and lets ash from it fall on the floor. He tears the letter in two. "I'll just file it away."

Both set-ups work, but what we have are two inherently different scenes. Either way, filmmakers, actors, and audiences want to feel emotionally involved with the people the scriptwriter has invented.

Speaking of the Stars

Compared with a novelist, the playwright and the scriptwriter have it easy. Whereas the novelist has to go it alone and write in all the nuances of character and utterance throughout the book, the play-wright and scriptwriter rely on actors to interpret their roles.

The industry annually lists the top box-office movie stars, which can be interpreted to read: the most bankable. Below is one list; the names will change from year to year, according to subsequent box-office success or decline. The average payment to anyone on the list hovers around the $10 to $20 million mark per picture. It doesn't take too much to understand the tremendous importance and value that a good screenplay has to these players.

- George Clooney
- Russell Crowe
- Tom Cruise
- Tom Hanks
- Brad Pitt
- Julia Roberts
- Will Smith
- Bruce Willis
- Reese Witherspoon
- Renee Zellweger

Star Power

Frequently, it is the star, the potential protagonist, who will be the most influential in getting a script off the ground and into produc-tion. Because this is an established method of raising the money for the budget, the description "bankable" came about. "So and so is a bankable star," it will be said, meaning, of course, that the star has clout in the business. Clout in Hollywood is earned and measured by box-office success, the sole criteria.

Stars and their advisors search endlessly for suitable scripts. Their reasons for choosing various projects change, but they are all searching for great roles. What is often not realized by the public is that actors and actresses who find that role will sometimes cut corners and take a cut in salary to play them. Remember, every actor wants an Academy Award. A-list actors want A-list directors and writers, but sometimes new writers and scripts squeak through. Great material has a way of opening doors. But the A-list shouldn't depress the average scriptwriter; there are hundreds of pictures produced every year, and certainly not all of them are star driven and made in Hollywood.

The Star as a Template

Although it is rare that the scriptwriter has the opportunity to actually write for a movie star, there is no harm in basing your protagonist on a specific actor—it will help you envision your character and the way he or she behaves and speaks. Many writers use existing stars as the template for the protagonist in a spec script. The hope is, of course, that the script is picked up by an agent who sees how well-suited the great script is to this big star, and the phones start humming.

Looked at from a creative point of view, there is a downside to the idea. You may be so taken up with a certain star that your script turns out to be a valentine to them. That is probably not going to work. If you objectively pick a star as a template, that might work; either way, you should act in exactly the same manner as you would when creating any protagonist.

Your first step on the research path is to establish whom you think might welcome a good script that was tailored for them; not all stars would. Check on stars who keep doing the same kind of picture, and check on those whose talents obviously outstrip the material they've been doing. That list might be a long one. Eventually, you will have narrowed your list down to a manageable size: if you're lucky, a list of one.

The best way to approach the project is not to get too involved in the idea that you are writing a script for a fabulous star. Just write the script the best way you can, as if you had penciled out a protagonist based on an amalgam of a couple of your friends. Don't sit at your keyboard trying to figure how Tom or Julia or whomever would handle a scene. Work out how your protagonist would do it.

Supporting Characters Shouldn't Hold You Up, but Help You Out!

The depth and strength of the supporting character is relative to his or her place in the plot. Many times a character acts as the foil for the protagonist, bouncing off or interacting with him or her. These characters stand out but don't detract from the protagonist's domination of the story and the screen. Famous comedy foils tend to act as the "feed" to their "straight" partner. Examples are: Abbott and Costello, Martin and Lewis, Laurel and Hardy, Will Smith and Tommy Lee Jones, Jim Carrey and Jeff Daniels.

Another manifestation of the supporting character is as the confidant (or confidante). The confidant is typically a close friend of the protagonist and privy to his or her private thoughts and problems. For the scriptwriter, this can be a useful device in that the protagonist can tell inner thoughts to the confidant without boring the audience with personal monologues. As you can see, having secondary characters can often help you solve the problem of sharing crucial information about what's going on without resorting to exposition or obviousness.

Supporting Characters: What We Can Learn

More than most, supporting players in movies, also known as character actors, easily become typecast; in fact with many that is their attraction. Hence the saying "He or she is right out of central casting." Audiences will frequently see the same actors or actresses turning up playing a similar part, although in a wide variety of pictures.

There are times when the supporting player in a film is considered to be the better actor/actress in the entire production. Some movie aficionados get to the stage of making their own list of their favorite supporting players. Here is a short one covering the years between 2000 and 2005—Oscar winners for best supporting actress:

2005: Rachel Weisz, *The Constant Gardener*
2004: Cate Blanchett, *The Aviator*
2003: Renee Zellweger, *Cold Mountain*
2002: Catherine Zeta-Jones, *Chicago*
2001: Jennifer Connelly, *A Beautiful Mind*
2000: Marcia Gay Harden, *Pollock*

And, for the same period, Oscar winners for best supporting actor:

2005: George Clooney, *Syriana*
2004: Morgan Freeman, *Million Dollar Baby*
2003: Tim Robbins, *Mystic River*
2002: Chris Cooper, *Adaptation*
2001: Jim Broadbent, *Iris*
2000: Benicio Del Toro, *Traffic*

Balancing the Characters

They don't have a category in the Oscars called Best Supporting Actor for nothing. That is a specific award title, which a person like Clint Eastwood has yet to win. Once that is well established in your mind, you can start thinking about balance. The balance needs to be between the protagonist and the supporting or "character" actors.

Major characters should have inner lives and a three-dimensional development. Major characters have emotional arcs. Ask yourself who are they when the movie begins, what happens to them, and how are they changed by it? Minor characters don't have to have an emotional arc, which isn't to say they are cardboard cut-outs. It's just that they generally don't have the same degree of depth.

In other words, they don't undergo any significant change, because they aren't involved in creating change in others or in events.

Try not to confuse a lack of change with shallowness. In fact, all speaking characters in a film should have personality! When you write your supporting characters, make sure that they don't run the danger of upstaging the protagonist. In your film, the protagonist has to remain the most developed character.

Extras and Bit Players

Depending on the type and breadth of a film, whether it's a sitting-room farce or a remake of *Gone with the Wind*, the number of actors will obviously vary. The bigger—or more extravagant—the film, the more "extras" will be needed. Extras are those people who provide "background presence," for instance, soldiers getting ready for battle or people walking by in the park. The demarcation line is between those who have lines to say and those who only have screen presence and don't speak.

The scriptwriter is not going to be too concerned about extras, just don't write *Ben Hur*. If your protagonist needs to walk through a picket line, all you'll need to write is the description line, something like "HARRY gets out of the cab and walks through the picket line." The director will be in charge of filling in the details. The picket line would be composed of extras, hired on a daily rate. The number of extras will have everything to do with budget.

Bit Players

Some characters are so minor, they may make a only single appearance in your screenplay. These characters are played by actors who do "bits," thus the title bit players. A bit player can deliver lines and gets paid accordingly. Unless the production is a low-budget flick, where some of the lines are made up as it goes along, the lines spoken by a bit player have to be written.

Look at the minor scene on the next page. If this quick scene makes it to the camera lens, you could bet that the actor playing the cabby is going to make the best of his two lines. (He'd like the director to notice how he was trying.) It has been known to happen that a director has liked a particular actor so much, he asked for another scene to be written for him.

Just because a character comes under the heading of a bit player doesn't mean a scriptwriter should dismiss the part and more or less write in anything just to fill space. Minor though it may be, the writer has the opportunity to make some kind of mark by writing dialogue, for instance, for a waiting cabby who does no more than just say, "Where to, sir?" You may keep this in mind as you write even the most minor characters—your work could start off the career of a small-role actor.

```
HARRY goes up to a parked cab and taps on its roof.
The CABBY looks half asleep; Harry taps again.

The CABBY opens one eye.

                    CABBY
          What's your problem?

                    HARRY
          Are you for hire?

The CABBY opens both eyes.

                    CABBY
          You see a sign that says open?
```

Naming Your Characters

The first step in creating dialogue for a character who stands a chance of actually remaining in the script is the character's name. While a rose by any other name may smell as sweet, if it could speak it wouldn't sound the same. Try dreaming up some off-the-wall names, then imagine what kind of dialogue you would write for characters with these names.

The names people have in real life frequently don't seem to fit them; have you ever met someone and later thought that they don't act and talk like a Bambi or a Rod? The language coming from a Blanche DuBois would probably not sound anything like the language coming from a Gertie Entwhistle.

Unless you are involved in writing an adaptation, where you are more or less obliged to use existing character names, give a lot of thought to the names you pick. Relate your choice to the kind of personality you want to project. Keep in mind that the language you eventually create for these characters should be closely allied to the kind of person they are meant to be. Most obviously, their names should signal their background. However, there are plenty of other ways to communicate information through a character's name. Nicknames work particularly well here, as do aliases. Quentin Tarantino found a creative way to use aliases in his film *The Reservoir Dogs*, where characters mask their anonymity with names like Mr. Pink, Mr. Blue, and Mr. Orange.

Dialogue: Defining Character

In the theater, words spoken onstage by actors are referred to as language. What you should learn is how language is spoken in films. Bad movie dialogue—and there's a lot of it—sounds as if the words were assigned, not spontaneously thought up by the character.

Good Dialogue Is Lean Dialogue.

Movies can entertain without words but they cannot exist without pictures. Therefore visuals must take precedence over dialogue. However, the power of dialogue cannot be underestimated. It is a crucial and necessary element of all good scripts.

- Dialogue reveals character and advances the plot.
- It conveys conflict.
- It communicates facts.
- It foreshadows impending events.
- It connects scenes and ties the pictures together.

How Does Good Dialogue Happen?

Where does it come from? Good dialogue comes from knowing your character, because character has its own voice. Rachel in *Friends* does not talk like Phoebe on *Friends*. They are very different characters; each of them has their own unique voice.

As far as I am concerned, rewriting is where all good dialogue happens. First draft dialogue exists to be rewritten. The rewrite is where it's honed, and trimmed. It's like the diamond that exists within the rock, but first all the excess must be chipped away. It is precise, economic, and mercilessly cut.

Hit Trick

"Screenwriters need determination to be original and an unwillingness to accept clichés. Most writers I know don't hesitate to change, or at least add something special as soon as they sense what they wrote has been done before." —Tom Schulman, screenwriter of **Holy Man, Medicine Man, Dead Poet's Society**, and **Honey I Shrunk the Kids**.

The late Paddy Chayefsky, one of our greatest television and feature film writers, and Academy Award winner for the movie *Network* said: "My own rules are very simple. First, cut out all the wisdom. Then cut out all the adjectives. I've cut some of my favorite stuff. I have no compassion when it comes to cutting. No pity or sympathy." Remember, if all good writers were doctors they'd all be surgeons.

Good Dialogue Is a Dance

Good dialogue is a dance of two and three-liners, a ball that keeps bouncing between characters. Is it real? Not really. But it gives the illusion of being real. If you went to your favorite fast-food place and recorded the actual conversation on tape and transcribed it, it would ramble, be wordy, and most likely very uninteresting. Aaron Sorkin, the creator of the *West Wing*, who is renowned for his sensational dialogue, says he looks at his dialogue as music. It has a natural rhythm and a tempo. We will take this into greater detail later in the book.

I can't tell you how often I hear "It was predicable." "The character had no surprises." "It was derivative, familiar; it's been done too many times before."

Clichés: Working with and Against Assumptions

Give the audiences what they don't expect. Surprise them. Stay away from stereotypes. Even the Godfather and Tony Soprano, who behave as stereotypical mobsters are very layered and complex characters who often surprise us.

It's an accepted fact that most of us form first cursory opinions about other people based on what are really a collection of marginal observations. Sometimes you can actually use this to your advantage and fool the audience. Let's say you have a male character who gives all the appearances of being a very upstanding, clean-cut, reliable sort of fellow. Don't overdo it and make him too good for words; instead, just make him a regular sort of guy, the type who would organize the local soccer league, or be active in his local church.

Then, write a scene in which this character hosts a dinner. The scene opens as the guests arrive. The audience sees the wife and maybe the children, before they scuttle out of sight. Everyone is having a great time and the impression is that this is a high-quality group of people.

At this point everything is open, and any kind of action can ensue. It's all in the hands of the scriptwriter. What's going on in the proper upper-middle-class house? Is it not quite what was first thought? Only the scriptwriter knows what'll come next.

Stereotypical Groups

The problem with the stereotypical character or group is that they themselves adhere to the established image. So what is the option if you want to write yet another Mafia flick? Maybe a WASP Godfather isn't going to work too well. Will the audience find this character believable? Or will the switch shock them out of the illusion of the film? Sometimes the decision to stick with stereotypes should depend on how realistic you want to be, whether you want to show true character or the dramatic one Hollywood would prefer.

What compounds the group cliché situation is that the groups tend to attach themselves to the image projected by movies; each feeds off the other until nobody knows who originated what. Probably the best a scriptwriter can aim for is to inject a new slant to the established stereotype.

Do Your Research

There is a frequent criticism written in reviews about some films that the characters—particularly minor roles and those of minorities or women—are one-dimensional. The critique is often justified. All characters matter!

It's important to do your research. The study of movies and screenplays help, but to really get at a character, you may want to go out and observe people. If you are writing a police detective story, try visiting the local police station. Really throw yourself into the experience like an actor does. Be careful, I had a partner once who got so carried away she ended up in jail! Writers need to be great observers, watch and listen; the world is your palate. The way to carry out successful research is to watch and listen. You can practice by writing characters who are diametrically the opposite of yourself. If you are a man in your fifties, try writing a teenage girl character. If you are a young woman, how about a character of an old man? Try changing the economic status, geographic location, and personality traits. If you stumble on a good character, you can use him or her in your screenplay.

Writing in the voice of someone else, completely different from your own, will force you to truly consider the ins and outs, likes and dislikes, weaknesses and strengths of your character. Put yourself in their shoes. See what happens, then write it down.

Chapter 7

Making It Interesting: Conflict and Dialogue

Conflict, Does a Movie Good!

Pick up any newspaper and you will find reports of immediate conflict. There is no getting away from it; countries have conflicts, as do people. The minute you start thinking about it and look inward, you can even find your own conflict.

Conflict is the cause of most of the trouble in the world, yours and everyone else's, but it can also provide great entertainment. Therefore, it's no wonder that conflict is at the heart of the dramatic structure. We all find it easy to recognize when we see it and most people can feel it coming. Looking at it from that point of view, it should not be too difficult for you to come up with some fine examples. They're all around you!

Major Conflict

Any minor conflict is still a conflict, but to drive the story along what you need most is "the major conflict," which is most often played out between the leading character and the antagonist. An intrinsic element of conflict is drama; without drama you will not have much in the way of conflict, because for it to manifest requires opposing forces. The two characters have to come up against each other; one option is to set up the plot so that the antagonist wants what the protagonist has—or vice versa. This struggle between the two characters is really all you need to serve as the basis for the creation of a major conflict.

But you don't necessarily need to pit two characters against each other to create a major conflict. The antagonistic force doesn't have to be a person. The following are a few examples:

> **Animals:** This approach has been in wide use ever since the *Godzilla* movies. More recent examples are *Anaconda* and *Jaws*.
>
> **Natural occurrences:** A tornado, a storm, an earthquake, and other natural disasters can serve to create conflict. For instance, in the film *The Perfect Storm*, the fishermen are pitted against the storm that threatens their lives.
>
> **World events:** Wars, revolutions, even elections all create sources of conflict. *In Saving Private Ryan*, World War II may be seen as the antagonist, or at least the antagonistic setting.
>
> **Things:** Ever heard the expression "man against the machine"? Yes, even objects can serve to create a major conflict. A good example is *The Matrix*. Can you think of any others?
>
> **The self:** Struggles between the protagonist and himself (or herself) are not an uncommon way to create conflict. *Fight Club* is a good example of how you can create a conflict of the self.

As you can see, virtually anything could create conflict. It might help to see conflict at work in literature. Take a look at the best of Stephen King (or maybe view some films based on his novels). King is a master at creating a combination of conflict with tension and suspense. Of course, he is not alone among writers at doing that.

Hit Trick

"Conflict is simply having characters not get what they want." —Leslie Dixon, screenwriter. Her films include, but are not limited to, **Hairspray**, **Just Like Heaven**, **Freaky Friday**, **The Thomas Crown Affair**, **Mrs. Doubtfire**, and **Loverboy**.

Minor Conflicts

It is very easy to slip into believing that all you need in a screenplay is a single conflict to get things going and to sustain the action for a hundred minutes or so. But that's not true at all, and a far cry from reality. While there may certainly be a single major conflict driving a film, there are always a number of other lesser manifestations.

For example, in a war film the major conflict is the war itself. But another, minor conflict may have to do with a soldier and his girlfriend back home—perhaps she's tired of waiting for her soldier or, on the contrary, the soldier meets a local woman while he's stationed in some foreign country. Surprisingly, in some circumstances one conflict can override another. To that soldier, the conflict with his girlfriend may temporarily become more important than the war.

A Secondary Conflict

Consider the movie *Witness*. The major conflict centers on the hardened Philadelphia detective John Book. Shortly after the death of her husband, Amish woman Rachel Lapp takes her son Samuel on a trip to Philadelphia. When young Samuel witnesses a murder in the train station bathroom, Book is on the scene. Book discovers that people within the police force are involved, and after being targeted himself and wounded he escorts Rachel and Samuel back to their home, where he stays to protect the boy while recovering. The bad cops that are hunting down Book and the boy are the major conflict. The secondary conflict is Book and Rachel who find themselves growing more and more attracted to each other, but both are aware that unless one of them is willing to leave behind their entire world, their love can never be. In the end the major conflict and the secondary conflict dovetail. In an action-filled end there is a gun battle of life and death, interwoven with a sensitive love story of caring and forbidden love.

Go Ahead, Meddle: Personal Relationships

On the face of it, it wouldn't seem too much of a stretch to come up with conflict in personal relationships. Many of us would only have to think about our own. All good writers are keen observers. Look at your world like a movie. Identify your own feelings and subtext. What is really happening inside you and what you are showing? If nothing else it will save you a fortune in therapy!

Writer Beware!

Many of the characters I have developed are based on real people. It's a great jumping off point. If you steal from real life, your creation will be identifiable to your audiences.

Love-and-Hate Plots

The ultimate conflict involves love and hate, two sides of the same coin. Frequently it is part of a family feud, brother against brother, sister against sister, blood against blood. Elia Kazan's *East of Eden* is based on the novel by John Steinbeck, which in turn is loosely based on the biblical story of Cain and Abel, and it is probably the most well-known "love and hate" plot line. The film was billed as being intense in its emotions and explosive in its passions. It was James Dean's first major motion picture; he played Cal—the bad brother modeled on Cain.

Set in the time of World War I, the story revolves around what would today be termed a dysfunctional relationship between Cal and his brother Aron (Abel, the "good" brother) in the rivalry for their father's affections. The father is of course Adam, played by the then-imposing Raymond Massey. Given some thought, it can be seen that the plot line of the Biblical story could very easily be adapted and brought into current times, which has frequently happened.

What held the audience in *Eden* was wondering how the major conflict would be resolved. Would Cal be reconciled with his father, and what would be the outcome for his brother Aron?

Like many Biblical plots, the Cain and Abel one is a classic. It is safe to say that the Bible, together with the works of William Shakespeare, provide a wonder chest of plot lines, most of them rich in conflict. It wouldn't hurt any aspiring scriptwriter, or even some successful ones, to study both collections.

Internal and External Conflicts

Personal relationships are a mix of internal and external conflicts. A good example is Shakespeare's *Macbeth* (there are two very good film versions: the Orson Welles version of 1948 and the Roman Polanski film of 1971). The murder of Duncan by Macbeth provides great psychological insights: Macbeth's inner turmoil before the murder and his external turmoil with Lady Macbeth both before and after it.

Films that concern themselves with brother/brother, sister/sister, and sister/brother relationships provide good movie fodder. Here are a few other examples:

- *A River Runs Through It*
- *Duel in the Sun*
- *In Her Shoes*
- *True Confessions*
- *The Brothers Karamazov*

Conflict Resolution

It is agreed that conflict is an essential ingredient of all dramatic work and comedy. It is conflict that audiences identify with, without it the story doesn't work. Conflict is the human condition; it only ends when we end. Even Forrest Gump, to whom life was like a box of chocolates, had great turmoil over Jenny!

The word conflict in the film industry has gained tremendous cachet, but, in doing so, a question has arisen: Has the weight of the word depleted the subtleties in a script or just become another over-used word?

Going to war is an issue of conflict and a creator of suspense: Will the lover/husband/wife come home and when? A divorce is the same, as is a trial for murder. But is missing the bus and being mad at the driver who wouldn't wait an issue? The answer must be relative to the individual. To a person with a short fuse it might well be an issue, a conflict, but not to Forrest Gump.

The scriptwriter has to tread a narrow causeway, one that goes between the dictates of the industry and the creativity of the artist. In many ways what is called a conflict is sometimes more of a mystery. If a character is late for an appointment, and the reason hasn't been given to the audience either verbally or visually, then that is a mystery to the audience. Creating mystery is good because it makes for involvement by the audience; they have a need to know the answer to the question, Why was he or she late?

Providing Clues Along the Way

It's probably not a good idea to keep the audience hanging around too much before they are at least given a clue as to the answer of a mystery. The clue, when it is given, should be just enough to pique their interest, such as, for instance, when the wife discovers under the front seat of her husband's automobile the cheap brooch that doesn't belong to her. What "sells" the answer is that the audience has seen that brooch on the "other woman" at an office party, as they know the wife must have.

In addition to conflict and issue, there's another word that might be considered: question. That is, question in the minds of the audience, not in a character in the film. Again, posing questions in the minds of the audience is an excellent involvement device. Will the hero catch his flight? Will his wife dump him? Will it rain on his parade?

It's therefore not a bad idea for a scriptwriter to arm himself or herself with a battery of these devices, all of which are designed to involve the audience: conflict, mystery, questions. They can be used either separately or together and might be brought out when the writer needs to create a plot point, either major or minor, or to heighten the attention of the audience for dramatic purposes. Keep them in your device arsenal.

Let's Talk About Dialogue

Dialogue in movies should contribute to the forward motion of the film. Good dialogue happens on two levels: what is being said and what is actually meant, or the subtext. As humans, we talk around things; we don't hit them on the head. In my early days of writing TV, producers and story editors would sometimes make a notation on my scripts, "too on the nose," or "fix it." I soon learned the phrase "on the nose" meant you are hitting the nail on the head, which in this case means there is no subtext.

What is subtext? It is what is happening under that which is being said, in other words, we don't go to someone's house and say "let's break up." As humans we often talk around it and try to finesse it, i.e., hide our true intent. We would say "I need more space," or "we should start seeing other people," but at the core, beneath the exchange, is the fact that we want out.

Hit Trick

"I read my dialogue out loud all the time. That's how you know if someone would really say something. If you can't say it, cut it." —Robin Swicord, screenwriter, coproducer, executive producer. Some of her films include **Memoirs of a Geisha**, **Matilda**, **Little Women**, and **The Red Coat**.

It has been said that writers either have an ear for dialogue or they don't. I believe to a certain extent this is true, but I believe this "ear" can be developed. You don't have to have perfect pitch to learn how to sing, it helps, but it isn't mandatory.

Try to hear dialogue as you write it, visualize the actors on the show delivering the lines, take an acting class, there are many ways to hone this skill.

Study common speech patterns and when you use them, try for consistency. All characters have their own voice. When you write the dialogue, avoid clichés, like the following gems:

- "It's quiet—too quiet."
- "I've been blind—blind, I tell you."
- "Oh, my God."
- "You look like you've seen a ghost."
- "Get your act together."

The problem with clichés and avoiding them is that with audiences they feel cozy, they are so familiar with them. After all, clichés were once phrases that worked very well in particular situations—so well, they were repeated over and over again until they gained their present status as trite and overused expressions.

The Reality of Cinematic Dialogue

When you are watching a movie, the conversations you hear onscreen sound pretty realistic. But if you were to compare them with real-life conversations, you'd realize that most of the time they're not so realistic. Real conversations have hesitations and repetitions. They break off and start up again, there are sudden shifts in topic, and often the speakers will go off-tangent and then forget what they were trying to say in the first place. Real dialogue is not reel dialogue. We all overtalk. Not so in the movies. Script dialogue must be lean dialogue that gives the illusion of being real.

Movie language is more focused and concise than your day to day language. This does not mean it is without subtext. It's subtle and layered but not rambling. Responses are shorter and monologues are discouraged. It's edited, rewritten, and spare, but natural.

Movie Influence

There are theories that movies affect society so much that people emulate them. There's been little doubt that fashion in movies has affected fashions in the marketplace. Behavior, too, is influenced by the movies, as well as television—particularly in teenagers. The same goes for speech; people say things the way they are said in movies. Remember "Show me the money" from *Jerry Maguire*? It is often difficult to know which came first, the real thing or the movie version.

Slang comes and goes and frequently originates in movies. Automobile sales are even influenced by films, the obvious example being the Aston Martin in the old Bond films. (Apparently they've changed brands to BMW.) The Mustang used in *Bullitt* not only gave the manufacturer some great exposure but provided the movie business with a lesson in how to film fantastic car chases; the one in *Bullitt* was shot on the hills of San Francisco and has ever since been endlessly copied.

"And . . . Action!": Get to Your Point

Good writing uses the active instead of the passive voice and is absolutely suited to writing for the movies. The active is more direct and vigorous than the passive. Writing in the active mode uses fewer words to say the same thing as in the passive: Mack was fired by Grant (passive); Grant fired Mack (active).

At the same time, you need to be as clear as possible. As some people in the business like to point out, writing a screenplay is not like writing a book. When we read, we always have the opportunity to go back and reread something we don't get the first time. But when you're in a movie theater watching a film, you can't just rewind and see the scene again. In a sense, there's only one first time in movies—the words are said, then they're gone.

Writer Beware!

There is no grammar to worry about in dialogue, because very few of us use correct grammar when we speak. Correct grammar sounds very pompous. Here's a well-known example from Sir Winston Churchill: "This is something up with which I shall not put." Ah . . . what was that?

Scenes today are much shorter than before. As mentioned earlier they shouldn't run to more than two or three pages, two to three minutes. Audiences want moving pictures. Like it or not we all have been desensitized and want everything faster. Film writers today break down long speeches and sequences by breaking up scenes. This means you change locales, start a new scene, or leave a scene before its natural conclusion. But remember, camera cuts are always the director's job, not yours. Directors make a point of routinely shooting cutaways, and using different camera angles.

Sound Like You Mean It: Vernacular

All professions have their own vernacular. If you happen to be at a cocktail party hosted by computer programming nerds, the odds are you might think you're in China for all you would understand of the conversation. When you create a character who is a computer programmer or a hacker, you'd better bone up on the computer vernacular, or that character is not going to ring true. You don't have to know a lot—just enough to convince the viewer of the character's authenticity.

The Vernacular of Class

As we all know, there is a vernacular of the social orders and it is in place throughout the world in one guise or another. Another way to put it might be to say that there is a pecking order wherever you go. For the purposes of looking at how this pecking order affects a screenplay and the characters in it, let's presume our illustration is the United States. Most people who have traveled in the United States are aware of how, in many ways, it is a continent made up of fifty different countries—if not more.

Each "country" has its own history of development and it even has its own particular laws. Certainly there is a wonderful selection of accents and ways of speaking. It follows that if you people your screenplay with a variety of characters from across the country, they must exhibit the many facets of their origins. Remember the fabulous characters and vernacular in *Fargo*? That wouldn't fly in Boston.

Telephone Conversations

Telephone conversations can be handled in a number of ways. First, you have to decide who is calling whom, then the purpose of the call and its emotional thrust, if any. The writer must also decide if they want to INTERCUT the conversation. That means see the people and locales at both ends. There is an example of an INTERCUT and how it is used in the script example from *The Harder They Fall*.

The Unseen Listener

If you decide your telephone scene will show only one of the characters, then you have to create a one-way conversation. Do not presume that you will be able to get away with the audience being able to hear the answers of the character on the other end of the phone.

(Not so with an answering machine, of course.) Write the scene knowing that you have to provide a one-way conversation from which the audience will be able to intuit what the unseen/unheard character answers.

A good way to research how you should write this kind of one-way conversation is to eavesdrop on cellular conversations people make in closed areas like bookstores, buses, trains, or in the theater.

On or Off Camera?

The 1959 film *Pillow Talk* with Doris Day and Rock Hudson is a romantic comedy that revolves around the two leads sharing a telephone party line. Naturally, they talk to each other without making a call; when they pick up their receivers to make a call, they find the other party has done the same, and so they end up talking to each other. Thus, the comedy form of the film title is established.

The point is that the film uses a split screen, Doris in one half, Rock in the other; they are both in their respective beds. It's a technique rarely used today, although in 1968 *The Thomas Crown Affair* with Steve McQueen and Faye Dunaway used multiple, virtually fragmented split screens. You, the writer, have to make these decisions: Do you want to show both parties or only one of them? If you decide on one only, which one—the one making the call, or the one receiving it?

"Here's Looking at You, Kid": The Line Everyone Remembers

You can write good dialogue, or you can try your hand at great dialogue and write lines that will be remembered and that your audiences will quote for years to come. *Casablanca* gave us a wonderfully written scene by the Epstein twins: Captain Renault and Rick (Claude Rains and Humphrey Bogart) are in conversation, and Renault is speculating on what brought Rick to Casablanca. Rick's answer is his health: "I came to Casablanca for the waters." Renault is surprised: "Waters? What waters? We are in a desert." Rick's answer is typically short and caustic: "I was misinformed." That is a scene everyone who has seen the picture remembers.

Many films have produced a line or a scene that instantly identifies the film. Ask anyone for the scene they remember most from *Butch Cassidy and the Sundance Kid*. Ask them which picture is famous for its shower. Even a single line can become part of the language. "Go ahead, make my day," uttered by Clint Eastwood's character Dirty

Harry, is an example. At the very end of *Some Like It Hot*, Jerry (played by Jack Lemmon), who had been masquerading as a woman, is in the boat of a rich suitor, played by Joe E. Brown. The suitor proposes, and Jerry then tells him he's a man. There's a pregnant pause and then the suitor retorts, "Well, nobody's perfect." Only three words, and it is one of the great last lines in a movie.

The Dazzle

How do those very special words and scenes come to be? Very often out of the blue, and probably more by luck than design. The writer is likely to be reaching for something—he or she doesn't know what it is, only that something is missing. Maybe it's just a couple of words, or one scene.

The motivating force behind all that is almost always a problem that needs to be solved. Writers shouldn't get nervous about problems—in fact, problems to be overcome very often lead to better results. Suddenly the idea comes and when it's written down on paper, the writer will look at the words on the page and—zappo—realize how right they are.

Chapter 8

Now, Making It Good: Communicating Your Purpose

A Different Type of Game: Show, *Don't* Tell

Exposition is "telling" or explaining as opposed to showing. Often exposition is done at the beginning of the film and this is where it is most acceptable. At its worst, exposition is having two characters tell each other information that, logically, they should already know. For instance, let's say a couple is swapping gossip about two of their mutual friends. But the whole point of the conversation is merely to clue in the audience about those two people, who may be introduced later. So, let's say Joan and Bill are having coffee. Joan says, "Did you hear that lovely Laverne is pregnant?" Bill replies, "Yeah, that's rotten. I guess that bastard Sam is the father." As you can see, this is too obvious of a ploy—not a good idea.

Your Job: To Show Everything!

Instead of relying heavily on exposition, what the writer should do is provide visual clues, which lets the viewers think for themselves. Avoid the temptation to "tell" the audience by using over written dialogue and unnecessary scenes to telegraph what the back story is about.

In *Love and Other Mayhem,* a movie I wrote with writer Jan Smith, Maggie and Joe grew up together as childhood enemies. They have lost contact with one another and are now adults. To better illustrate "show" don't "talk," here, we pick up on page 5 of the screenplay:

```
INT. JOE'S NEW APARTMENT - SAME

The apartment is piled high with boxes. A pretty woman in her
midtwenties, LINDA, Joe's wife, is unhappily staring out the
window. JOE, now twenty-six, looks like a pack mule as he car-
ries more boxes inside.

                    LINDA
          We left Boston for this?

                     JOE
          Honey, this is where I grew up. Seattle's
          a great town, you'll see. You're going to
          fall in love with it.

Linda looks back at the downpour; she's not so sure about that.

EXT. DOWNTOWN SEATTLE - SAME

CRASH! The storm takes out the electrical grid in sections,
boom, boom, boom, the ENTIRE CITY GOES BLACK!

INT. MAGGIE'S HOME - SAME It's PITCH BLACK inside.

                MAGGIE'S VOICE
          Great, there goes dinner.

FITZZZ! A match is struck. We expect Joe or Linda, but see
Maggie's mature, twenty-six-year-old face instead. She lights
candles on the kitchen table. The only thing on it is a bottle
of wine.

                    MAGGIE
          What do we do now?
```

Her husband, CLIFF, comes up and nuzzles her. He eyes the wine, a smile slowly comes over his face.

> CLIFF'S VOICE
> Do you know what happens during a blackout, Mrs. Kennedy?
> He kisses her neck. She smiles and leans into him.

> MAGGIE'S VOICE
> I can't imagine, Mr. Kennedy. What does happen after a blackout?

SMASH CUT

EXT. HOSPITAL - FULL MOON

At the HOSPITAL entrance a car door flies open. Inside, a very PREGNANT MAGGIE is about to deliver.

> CLIFF
> MAGGIE, WAIT!

But she's not going to wait on anything or anybody, this baby's coming and she's got to get inside! He jumps out after her.

EXT. CITY GRID - SAME

A SIXTEEN-WHEELER has overturned and blocks a major artery into the hospital. The FIRE DEPARTMENT is cleaning up, the CHP's directing traffic . . . only a single lane is open but it's barely moving.

A mile down the road, Joe sticks his head out of one of the cars.

> JOE
> MOVE IT PEOPLE!

INSIDE he lays on the horn wondering what in heck is the hold up. Next to him, Linda is just as pregnant as Maggie. She gets an overwhelming contraction.

> LINDA
> JOE!!!!!!!

Desperate, Joe finds an opening and exploits it. He pulls to the right and squeezes between the cars on his left and a concrete barrier on his right and heads for the hospital laying paint the whole way.

INT. HOSPITAL EMERGENCY ROOM - SAME

The RECEPTION area is in utter chaos. It seems the blocked traffic has impacted everybody; people wait for someone to take them in, but there's a shortage of staff due to the backup. On the wall, a television SHOWS THE BOTTLENECK AND OVERTURNED RIG.

INT. MATERNITY WARD

Maternity's just as busy as the rest of the hospital. NURSES, DOCTORS, pregnant women, and clueless husbands jam the hallways. The doors blow open AND MAGGIE BARRELS THROUGH.

> MAGGIE
> Out of the way! Out of the way!

A second later Cliff runs in pushing an empty wheelchair. He catches up to Maggie and scoops her into the chair.

> CLIFF
> Relax, honey. Remember what they said, it's
> just pressure, not pain, pressure not --

Maggie gets a contraction, reaches back and grabs his arms.

> MAGGIE
> My uterus is launching into outer space
> without me and you call this pressure!

Her nails dig into his skin. He grimaces in pain.

EXT. HOSPITAL ENTRANCE

We see Joe and Linda arrive. Joe has to maneuver around Cliff's abandoned car.

>   JOE
>   Idiot!

INT. MATERNITY - SAME

A harried DOCTOR, DR. CHARLIE LEIB, puts on her scrubs as she and a FEMALE NURSE and a MALE NURSE head toward DELIVERY.

>   FEMALE NURSE
>   Full moon, I knew I should have called in
>   sick. This is insane!

>   DR. LEIB
>   This is you in a few months.

The nurse touches her belly, we see now that she is expecting. She looks askance at a screaming woman being wheeled past.

>   DR. LEIB (cont'd)
>   Nowhere to run, nowhere to hide.

IN ANOTHER HALLWAY
Cliff is running with Maggie.

Maggie reaches out and grabs a MAINTENANCE MAN by the collar. He drops his mop and pail.

>   MAGGIE
>   Morphine! I need morphine!

>   CLIFF
>   Sweetie, he's not a doctor.

As the maintenance man is being dragged along, Cliff tries to extract the poor man from her grip. Maggie BITES him. Cliff yells as all three of them disappear into the delivery room.
[ENDEXT]

What have we learned with very little dialogue?

1. Seattle had a blackout.
2. We cut to nine months later and SEE the result of it. Maggie is pregnant and about to deliver. So are a lot of women. This is a phenomenon that happens after blackouts.
3. To add to the chaos there is a full moon and a truck has overturned blocking a main artery to the hospital. We discover that Joe is in one of the cars with his wife who is just as pregnant as Maggie.
4. The women are about to deliver at the same time. The doctors are hurried and the nurses exhausted.

In the script we pick up Joe and Maggie ten years later, both are single parents and they will discover that they have been raising each other's babies.

Communicate: Metaphors, Flashbacks, and Voice-Overs

Another way of communicating meaning is by relying on symbols and metaphors—literary devices that work by way of comparison. For example, some years ago, I returned from Portland, Oregon, where I was a keynote speaker. I had a great two-day stay and my talk went extremely well. I arrived at the airport very late at night still dressed from a party I had attended. The man I was dating had come to the airport to pick me up. He was grubby, unshaven, and had been packing for relocation all day.

On the ride home from the airport, I excitedly told him about my successful trip. Mid sentence he cut me off and said, "Look for a Seven-Eleven, I've got to find trash bags." What he really was saying was "I don't want to hear about it." The trash bags were a metaphor and subtext for "I don't want to hear anymore."

He didn't say "I'm under an incredible amount of stress, and I've been packing all day." Why? Because in the context of our relationship I already knew that. Just as in the context of the script we would already know it. The metaphor was the trash bags, and the subtext was very discernible.

Using Flashbacks and Voice-Overs

Two techniques we are all very aware of are flashbacks and voice-overs (V.O.), to help with exposition. The flashback takes us visually back to an earlier time. The voice-over is narration over a picture or pictures.

In *The Usual Suspects*, written by Christopher McQuarrie, flashbacks and voice-overs are used to tell the story. The film star Verbal (Kevin Spacey), an eye-witness and participant who tells the story of events leading up to the police investigating an exploded boat on a San Pedro pier and $91 million worth of drug money.

This Academy Award–winning screenplay is filled with suspense, intrigue, and lots of twists in the plot.

In the classic *To Kill a Mockingbird*, the movie opens with Scout's voice as an adult woman recalling her past in the south. It creates the entire tone of the film. Some of my favorite films have flashback and voice-overs, and the screenplays were greatly enhanced by their use. The problem is most beginning writers use these techniques poorly— that is, only as a device to get needed information out and that's why they are often a signpost of novices and poor writing. Make sure to keep this in mind when you're giving it a shot!

A Newsreel

Citizen Kane uses both techniques within the device of a newsreel being shown in a projection room. This is early on in the picture, immediately after the Rosebud sequence with the glass ball and Kane's deathbed shot. It is obvious that we are watching a newsreel that has been compiled to illustrate Kane's career. A man's voice starts the voice-over narration.

As the newsreel ends, the lights come up in the projection room. A discussion takes place about the newsreel and it is decided that another angle is needed that tells not only what Kane did but also who he was. On that premise the picture proper begins, as a reporter starts his investigation.

The newsreel technique, which is very effective, would today, of course, be done by a simulated television news program. And, as has been done in other pictures, it would quite probably use real-life commercial news anchors. The point here is that this kind of production device can add tremendously to the verisimilitude of the picture.

Moving the Story Forward

In *Sunset Boulevard* (1950), flashbacks and voice-over narration are used to tell the story. The film stars William Holden as Joe Gillis and silent-screen star Gloria Swanson as Norma Desmond. German film director Erich von Stroheim plays Norma Desmond's valet/chauffeur and former husband. It was written by Charles Brackett, Billy Wilder, and D. M. Marshman, Jr. The picture received rave reviews and Wilder won an Academy Award for Best Story and Best Screenplay.

Wilder took a big gamble in that he had the picture open at the end of the story and used the voice of Gillis, who is dead, to narrate the film, more or less start to finish (or perhaps it should be said, from finish to finish). The original start was of shots of Gillis in the morgue talking, voice-over, of course, to the other bodies in the morgue. The bodies answer back and explain how they got there. Apparently preview audiences were so put off by the sequence that it was cut.

The final cut version opens with a close-up shot of a street sign, Sunset Boulevard, stenciled on a curbstone. Police sirens are heard and policemen and newspaper reporters are seen crowding around a disused swimming pool. There is a body floating facedown in the pool. A man's voice is heard: "Yes, this is Sunset Boulevard, Los

Angeles, California. It's about five o'clock in the morning. . . ." The voice is that of William Holden. He starts to tell how he got to be dead in the pool.

Hit Trick

"Sometimes you can have something you might call 'pure entertainment,' and theme is not very important. But if you want more than just entertainment, if you want to entertain, and enrich, and inspire, or say something about the world and the human condition, then you have to think about what you want to say in order to subtly weave it through the story." —Gerald DiPego, screenwriter and producer. His movies includes, but are not limited to **Phenomenon**, **Angel Eyes**, **Message in a Bottle**, and **Instinct**.

The shot changes to show a view of Hollywood and some apartments. The voice-over continues and tells us what he used to be, a scriptwriter, where he was living, and that he wasn't doing too well. There is another shot change to the interior of an apartment. It's not very spacious nor affluent looking. Joe Gillis is sitting on the edge of a pullout bed typing. The doorbell sounds.

At that point the story/film starts its new chronological order. Gillis gets up and opens the door. Two men have come to repossess his car. After some chitchat the two men leave. The voice-over starts up again to explain what is going on in his life, which isn't too much. Gillis picks up his car, which has been parked in a back lot. He goes to Paramount Studios; all the time the voice-over continues telling the audience what's going on.

We are now into the picture proper and while there are a few more incidents of voice-over sequences, the film then proceeds. The technique reappears whenever it's necessary to fill the audience in on what's in Gillis's mind. This continues right to more or less the very end with Gillis back in the pool floating facedown. In spite of the production technique being totally illogical—a dead man telling how he got that way—the film was a tremendous critical and box-office success.

Hit Trick

"The answer to any problem pre-exists. We need to ask the right question to reveal the answer." —Jonas Salk, an American physician and researcher, best known for the development of the first polio vaccine.

"What's Going to Happen?": Keep 'Em Guessing

Telegraphing means exactly that, letting the audience know what's coming next instead of holding it back. For example: A character states "I am going to the store," and then the locale changes and guess where they are—the store. This totally negates the beauty of film where you can just visually go there and let the audience see it for themselves. Show, don't talk about. Let the audience get caught up in the discovery process.

Cliché-Ridden Scenes

If you've seen it a thousand times, don't write it! If you are ever tempted to write it anyway, just to make it easy on yourself, shame on you! Work at doing something fresh. Try to do something unique and original. Trust me, when writers do this in Hollywood they are spotted. One way writers stand out is through their dialogue. Since characters should have their own voice, you might wonder what I mean by this. The dialogue is consistent to the character, but it sings. Take writers like Aaron Sorkin, *A Few Good Men* and creator of *The West Wing*, and Alan Ball, *American Beauty* and *Six Feet Under*.

Writer Beware!

Get into the habit of reading your work from the point of view of what you can cut. Ask yourself what is unnecessary? Do I need to show it at all? What is the story really about? It wasn't about? Joe and Maggie growing up together and their ten years apart were not the story. It was the hook that they were raising each other's babies, therefore we cut an entire ten years out of the script.

If you can write dialogue like this, Hollywood will find you. Charlie Kaufman is a great example of a writer who uses original and edgy dialogue. Look for some of his best work in the movies *Being Inside John Malkovich*, and *Adaptation*. Hollywood isn't as stupid as you think; even if something they write isn't commissioned, great scripts get sent around town. That writer is put on a "recommend" list and people keep their eyes on them. Even when scripts don't sell, and that is often, great ones open the door to an eventual sale.

Elements of Suspense and Tension

Withholding information is a key tool in creating suspense. Why? Because it keeps the audience in the discovery process. When I first broke into television I wrote a segment on *Fantasy Island*. The story was about a brother and sister who go back to the island to relive a terrible night in their childhood to solve a parent's murder. The script was basically a mystery and loaded with clues. The story editor at the time, Larry Forrester, read my treatment and said I laid out too much information, too fast. I needed to go back and pull out information (exposition) and then slowly plant it throughout the script— letting the audience know one thing but always withholding something else. It worked beautifully and I have been doing it ever since.

Try to keep the telling to an absolute minimum. Audiences love to get involved. Let them put the pieces together.

The Value of Keeping Quiet

Silence is the ally of tension and suspense; couple it with controlled time and you can create high tension. Time elongates and contracts itself on film, and this is something the scriptwriter can take advantage of. To learn the power of silence and film pacing rent some suspense pictures—*Psycho* would be one good choice—and watch them on your VCR and time them. Be prepared to stop and rewind segments.

Find the sequence in *Psycho* where the private detective goes into the house late at night in an effort to talk to the mother, the scene where he starts going up the stairs. Time the silence from the beginning of the shot up to the point where the musical effect tells us that Mother with her knife is coming. Analyze the scene and the emotions it generates.

The silence greatly contributes to the tension. When you get ready to do this, keep in mind that Hitchcock was a master of this kind of emotional manipulation. You couldn't have a much better tutor. In fact, you could emulate what some famous directors have done by going through the list of Hitchcock thrillers and spending your spare time studying them. It will be time well spent.

Test It Out

The power of silence works in all genres, not just mystery. It is crucial in comedy for delivery and pacing. Study movies and see how often it is used. You will be astounded. A good exercise is to go back to one of your dialogue scenes and rewrite it with this in mind. Ask yourself where are the spaces? Can I show this? Does the character have to respond? It is a wonderful device and what film is all about. They say of the great play/scriptwriter Harold Pinter that he had mastered the art of writing the silences. The masters of fine art always work with the vacant spaces.

Tension in *Body Heat*

Tension is a subject that can be neither overstressed nor overdone. In the movie *Body Heat* the tension is powerful. Ned Racine finds Mattie Walker at an outdoor concert on a very hot Florida night. She's aloof, but enticing. From all indications she is unhappily married, very rich, and sexually unfilled. She is the quick score the lazy attorney has been looking for. Mattie disappears and Ned becomes obsessed with finding her. He finally does at a neighborhood bar. She allows him into her home, but it's only to see the chimes on her patio. When he goes to kiss her she locks him out but taunts him through the window. Ned can't take it any more and breaks through a plate glass window to get to her. From this point on Mattie convinces him to kill her husband. In Act 3 Ned will realize he has been set-up for the crime. At each turn we are on the edge of our seat watching Mattie, waiting for her next move, and then discovering with Ned that this was her plan all along.

Did You Hear Something? It's Not Just Noise

Such is the power of movies that many young people know more about how movies and television programs play out than they do about current events, geography, and a number of other topics previously thought to be common knowledge. Modern audiences are watching films in greater numbers than ever before, not only in the cinemas, but also on television, videotapes, and DVDs. In the process, they have become educated as to what to expect from films. Dating from somewhere around the introduction of MTV and its frenetic crosscutting, the technique of speed editing found its way into film production and strongly influenced the way modern films are made. As a result, we've got what might be called the "short attention span" audience. Unfortunately readers in Hollywood have a similar short attention span. I watched *Rear Window* the other night and I am ashamed to say I found it slow. Not that it wasn't brilliant, but today I promise you it would be a hard sale.

The Elements of Holding Back

Writers are learning that because film audiences know about movies, there is no need to send messages ahead to tell them what's on its way; these messages can be either verbal or visual. For instance, in the old days the setup might be an urchin hanging about and a posh business-type coming out of his house. He is wearing a blue pinstripe suit and a bowler hat, and he carries a briefcase.

The urchin has a banana that he starts to peel. The posh man keeps coming, his nose in the air. The urchin is eating the banana. Still the businessman keeps coming. The urchin throws the banana peel over his shoulder and walks off. The posh man doesn't see the banana. He steps on it, his legs go from under him, and he ends up on his rear end. (Predictable result: Audience laughs.)

Today, because audiences are film-educated, all that is needed are the setup and four shots: Posh man comes out of his house. Urchin is eating a banana. Urchin walks away. Posh man's legs go out from under him and he lands on his rear end. (Predictable result: Audience laughs.) The audience has filled in what wasn't there. You don't have to show all the details.

Writer Beware!

There are sounds in the modern productions that don't exist until a film goes into production. For instance, in **Return of the Jedi**, which is part of the Star Wars trilogy, a laser gun might be fired. The sound had to be invented and now appears in the sound library, to be used in other movies.

Paying Attention to Sound

A screenwriter must think beyond physical images and words to be spoken. Just as audiences will vary considerably in their opinions about a picture up on the screen, so a reader in an office evaluating screenplays will, in principle, be doing the same thing to the pages on a desk.

Most of the sound heard coming from a film in a cinema appears to be real; much of it isn't, and even if it is, it is frequently manipulated. The majority of the sound recorded on location will have to be recreated and rerecorded in the studio, then eventually mixed with all the other sound tracks: dialogue, music, ambient sound, and so on.

Indicating Sounds

The text on the pages has to conjure up pictures in action complete with sounds. Writing a script to format means it is necessary to type in block caps the important actions and sounds. Remember that included in the list of people who will need a copy of your script are the sound technicians; they have to come up with the sounds.

When you write direct indications of important actions and sounds, you can set them in caps, but even this is becoming a bit outmoded. I will capitalize only when it is absolutely important. Otherwise, it can get monotonous to the reader. You never should do anything too much because it gets tedious. Always remember that the sounds should have a direct relevance to character and place.

Getting Attention

As you know, sound effects can play a major part in films. Sounds in movies are manipulated so well that the viewer gets heavily involved in listening very carefully to the picture. Below are a few examples of sounds and actions that might appear in your script:

- The door slams shut.
- The wheels of the car SCREECH.
- Jazz music is coming from. . . .
- He shoots him dead.
- Everyone is SHOUTING.
- The door slowly squeaks open.

Use the caps with discretion, but do mention important sounds that will be put in by the sound tech. Sounds like a phone ringing don't happen on the set, they are placed in later.

How do scriptwriters deal with overlapping dialogue and/or sounds? They may use ellipses (. . .) to indicate an interruption, or at the beginning of an utterance to indicate partial dialogue as it comes into earshot.

Using Music As Background

There is another way in which sounds can be used either in conjunction with words or without them: music. It's good to add music into your screenplay, as long as you are careful. You should never write in the name of a song or of a particular artist. However, you can indicate a type of music coming from a CD player or a television, to create a feeling or tone. If character is listening to loud rap, that tells us something. The name of the song and the rapper is not important and should be left out. I recently completed a screenplay entitled *The Swing Sisters* about the first female integrated band during WWII. Essentially the piece is a *League of Their Own* to music. In this case mentioning and suggesting certain tunes was very important for the feel of the times. It was important in *American Graffiti*. In play *Misty for Me* the song held the clue. But again use discretion. If a couple dances to a waltz, don't tell us which one unless it is imperative to the story.

Generally speaking, background music is not in the domain of the screenwriter. The composer of the film will pick up emotional cues from the script and write the score. This is their job and a very important one. Can you name a great film that didn't have a great score? It's hard.

Chapter 9

A Life of Its Own: Reeling It In

Discipline, Not Just for Kids

Without any discipline, a writer is not going to get far. Although it would be great, it is not true that you can sit at the keyboard and channel Orson Welles. You actually have to work. Once you start this writing game, you will develop a rhythm to your day. If you have the luxury of choosing any part of the day or night to write, think about your style and your personality. Are you a morning person or a night person? Do you need structure and discipline to move forward with a project, or are you more easygoing—you always get the job done, but you don't follow any rules?

Make the Time to Write

Even with the busiest schedule, you can still carve out hours of time for writing. Some writers find they can do their best work only at a certain time of day; others learn that they can start their engines whenever a free hour surfaces. Some of these authors establish a certain number of hours each day that they must ply their craft. Others determine that they must write a certain number of words or pages at each session. Through writing you'll settle on your own best schedule and writing-output goals. But you have to put in the time to find your answer.

If your life is already filled with career, family, volunteer work, and extracurricular activities, you can still find time to write. It may be hard, but you can do it. Consider getting up a bit earlier than you usually do, if you're a morning person. Night-lifers will find it easier to head to the writing table after dinner or after everyone else has gone to bed. Instead of going out to lunch every day, just about everyone can brown-bag it, close the office door (or go to the library or a park), and set aside that time to write. On weekends, try setting aside a bigger block of time to create.

Think about enlisting friends or family members who might be able to take over chores for you or who you might be able to trade services with. You can also hire a baby-sitter, dog walker, gardener, or such to free up some time for you to write; the expense may be high, but the cost to you of not writing may be higher. By sitting down and really studying what you do and when you do it, you'll likely find some daily time that you can dedicate to your craft.

Developing a Writer's Routine

It's important to create a sense of routine. In some writers, this borders on superstition. For instance, some people will use only a certain kind of pencil for writing. Others won't begin until they've got their favorite coffee mug filled with coffee. Even if you're working at home, you can create a certain sense of work time, as if you are actually leaving your home and going to the office. This kind of routine contributes to a writer's well-being and helps her or him to feel comfortable with the creative process.

Writer Beware!

Remember, you are in charge of your schedule. As long as you set up a good time to work, it doesn't matter whether it's in the middle of the night, early in the morning, or in the late afternoon. What matters is that you have a set amount of hours during which you expect to get some work done.

Set up Your Workplace

In many authors' experience, surroundings and equipment that suit their personalities and styles make it more likely that the blank page before them will eventually be covered with compelling writing. In fact, the ideal writing place may automatically, just by your being there, set your writing muscles in motion.

What would work for you if you had the luxury of setting up a custom workplace? Think about how you like to read or study, how sound affects you, how easily you're distracted, how disciplined you are, if you need people around you, and your general nature.

It will work well, if you have the space, to set aside part of where you live in which to work. Tell everyone, particularly children and animals, to keep away and not to touch anything, under fear of retribution. (Always number your pages.) If it's possible, leave your working pages out on the table; don't be overly tidy. Then in the morning, eyes open, coffee cup in hand, dressing gown tied, drift by the table.

You will typically look down at the odd page or two and something will catch your eye. That's when you do an edit. At night, or whenever you decide to stop work, take some advice from Mr. Hemingway: "Always stop when you know what comes next." If you do that the odds are you will never get what some people call "writer's block"—running out of what to say.

Your Personal Style

Because making a motion picture is such a collaborative business, it would seem unlikely that different styles could emerge. And yet, there are some films that are so distinctive, you can name the writer without referring to the credit list. Sooner or later, a good craftsman will develop a style. A style can only be experienced, learned, or copied—it can't be taught.

Taken to the extreme, some actors develop a style that they reproduce in every film they do. When that happens, it is said that they have become typecast. A distinctive style is also seen in the work of many directors, with the most obvious example being Alfred Hitchcock.

In filmmaking these days, the power is overwhelmingly in the hands of the directors. So, for a writer to develop a distinctive style, it is probably wise to work toward having a style that is aimed at appealing to directors. Thus, a certain director may like your particular style and seek you out for his or her next production. As time goes by, your style will then stand a chance of being recognized, at least in the business if not with the public.

The Magic of Billy Wilder

It was three men whose collaboration produced a virtually endless list of wonderful pictures. The writer and director Billy Wilder led this group. In 1942 Wilder began collaborating with another writer, Charles Brackett, in their work at Paramount Studios. Together, the two men produced *The Lost Weekend* and *Sunset Boulevard*, both of which earned Oscars for best screenplay. After *Sunset Boulevard* Wilder left the partnership and took up with another writer, I. A. L. Diamond. Together they produced *The Apartment*, which won Oscars for best picture, director, and screenplay. Both men were also responsible for *Some Like It Hot*. Billy Wilder was probably the last of the major writer/directors to come out of Hollywood; twenty-five major films list Wilder as the director and cowriter. In his later years, into his nineties, he continued to go to his small office in Beverly Hills to work.

The Three Rs: Review, Revise, and (Even) Rewrite!

You are creating a work that you might think of as your baby. You've sweated over it on your own. You know what it's like to be a writer facing a blank screen or a blank piece of paper. Maybe a year has gone by and at last you have the 120 pages of your final draft stacked in front of you. And someone is telling you it needs work? Listen to them, maybe it does. Put the draft aside and go fishing for a day or two. Think about your possible career in the screenwriting business. Come home and think again about the advice. After all, it is your first screenplay.

Everyone works in a different manner; one way to deal with the necessity of editing is to give yourself some distance from the script. When you finally reach the finish line, don't write FADE TO BLACK and then turn the pages back to FADE IN on the same day. Take a break; go shopping—hey, chop wood in the rain if that's what it takes. In fact, do anything but rewrite that script. It is important that you try to get some time and distance before you go back and reread your work. But don't think you're done! After the first draft, some people even say it's just the beginning.

The Power of Rewriting

To improve your first draft, you will need to rewrite. Your motive during this process must be to make your screenplay better. Know in advance that there are going to be weaknesses in your work, everyone does.

It's a very good idea to have a strong element of humility toward your work. If you need inspiration, view any of the finest movies you can rent and study their screenplays. Try to pick out the scenes that really stun you, then ask yourself, how did they do it? Then look for your own weaknesses in your script; find what doesn't work. Look at every scene that doesn't move the story or a character development forward. When you find it, cut it; learn to be ruthless.

Writer Beware!

Remember: The first draft of anything is just that, a first draft. Now you have to start doing the real work. In scriptwriting it is estimated that three scripts have to be completed before you know what you are doing. This may be one reason why many people don't make it in the business.

If you can't see your scenes visually, something is wrong. Don't write the words so they "tell" the reader/viewer what is going on; the words have to be employed in "showing" what is happening.

Let's take a look at an example. Your description line could read: "Jason looks at the candle. It goes out. He stands back against the wall. His hand moves to his holster. The door creaks. He pulls out his gun and cocks it." This kind of writing shows what is going on, and from the action we can infer what is happening inside the character as well. He's cautious, perhaps scared, and he's ready for action. Read the passage again. Does it help you visualize what is going on?

How Film Editing Relates to Written Editing

In literature and journalism, "editing" is the process of rewriting, but in film it's the editing of the 35mm film—it used to be that the editing process meant cutting and gluing together pieces of film. That's why "editing" in film isn't used to refer to the process of rewriting. Instead, the script drafts are known as rewrites.

However, both rewriting and editing have more in common than might first be thought. It all depends on when the function is done. If you are writing a spec script, then the rewriting is probably going to be done before almost anyone else sees the finished product. The editing of a film typically takes place when the shooting and tampering with the script is over.

And, of course, there are times when someone in power orders up retakes or the scripting and shooting of new scenes in an effort to either improve or save a film. A general clue, incidentally, as to whether or not a film has been in trouble is the number of screen-writing credits on the finished product. If you see three or more writers credited, it's a fair chance something was wrong; of course, often the writers brought in to "doctor" a script aren't credited.

Be confident though. Don't let yourself become so cynical that you believe that once your spec script has been bought, it will immediately go out for rewrites by some other writer and so there's no need to bother doing rewrites yourself. Subjectivity reigns. Which means that much of the rewriting by others is aimed not at improvement but at change. This change is to suit the opinion of someone else. There are people out there who would change anything just to put their seal on it.

The Rewriting Process

When you sit down at your keyboard or typewriter, you should be able to visualize in your mind's eye what the words are saying. Is there a better way to say it? A more concise way? Lean is the name of the game in film.

Let's presume you have achieved a reasonable amount of objectivity about your script. You know what it is supposed to do and how. You first check the structure, making sure that the three acts, plot points, and such, are in the right places and do their job. When you started out writing the screenplay, you had a very good idea in mind about what it was you wanted to accomplish.

Hit Trick

"I rewrite a lot more than anyone would think. I believe the difference between a professional and a beginner is that while they both write a lot of crap, the professional knows it and knows when to show it. It's just about editing more effectively." —an American screenwriter Ed Solomon. His movies include, but are not limited, to **Men in Black**, **Super Mario Bros**, **Leaving Normal**, **Bill and Ted's Bogus Journey**, and **Bill and Ted's Excellent Adventure**.

Now that you've reached the end, it's time to go back and check to see if you have achieved your original purpose. It's not unlikely that your purpose got lost along the way—if that's the case, don't get discouraged. Instead, try to figure out ways of how best to fix this problem.

Cut It Out!

Probably the most difficult part of rewriting is deciding on what has to go. After all, it's your baby that's being considered; you have sweated for hours over its prose, dialogue, and images, and now, you wonder in dismay, something has to be cut? Why, you might ask, is it necessary to consider cutting? Perhaps your script runs to 140 pages, so at least twenty-five of those have to end up in the trash can.

But there are other reasons as well. It could be that your second act is too slow, or that the transition from the first to second act just doesn't work. Or it may be that a secondary character is just not working and you need to consider cutting him out completely, and possibly replacing those scenes with something else. Whatever the case may be, you have to sit down and make some hard decisions.

Go With Your Gut

As you make cuts, there is something very important to consider—your intuition. It is said that the more you rely on it, the stronger it will become. Look at it from this point of view: You read over your pages and you suddenly get a gut feeling; that's your intuition. When what you have just read over doesn't seem to scan quite right and something seems wrong with it, generally your gut feeling is right—there is something wrong with it.

Once you start cutting, you'll feel like a weight has been lifted from your shoulders. If you are worried about cutting, always remember that you can save your original files or copies and can always go back to them if you don't like your changes. Nothing will be gone for good, unless you don't save the old versions.

Reviewing Your Dialogue

A problem that can come about in writing dialogue is being able to tell if it "plays," meaning if it works. An actor may often turn from a page of script and say, "It doesn't play." What this means is that either the rhythm is off in some way or that some of the words are not easy to deliver.

Reading over your own work to evaluate it is never easy, and this is especially true when it comes to reading dialogue. One method you might adopt is to record your dialogue on a portable tape recorder and play it back to yourself. Try to give yourself some distance from the time you made the recording to the time you listen to it—that'll help with your objectivity. Ask yourself: How does it sound? Is it right for the characters? Does it sound like them? Is the dialogue "written on the line," which means, does it say what it means?

If you are lucky enough to have a companion or friend who is interested in what you're trying to accomplish and willing to get involved, then you might see if they would read the lines with you and maybe even act them out. If you have kids and the film is not inappropriate for their reading, you may want to have them re-enact your scenes—they'll enjoy it just as much as you will!

Get Feedback

Showing your first draft around in a cozy writing group may seem like a good idea, and it is—until you suddenly find some of your smart dialogue being read back to you from someone else's script. One method that can work is to read and play out your script to a movie-going friend. Pick a friend who likes the kind of films that are close to what you've written.

Hit Trick

"Ask advice from everyone, but act with your own mind." —Anonymous

In other words, perhaps don't risk your high-energy murder mystery on a person who thinks *The Sound of Music* was the greatest film they've ever seen. Before casting your pearls around, first take a good hard look at your proposed recipient. Let's say you have already established that they like your kind of movie. But, what else might be a factor in their opinion? Well, their gender, for one: There are boy films just as there are girl films.

Be Aware of the Risks

There's a very good reason for going to all this trouble finding the right audience for your first draft. It's called rejection. Rejection, as you must know, is someone telling you that your wonderful screenplay is not quite what he or she is looking for. The fact that this person probably didn't know what he or she was looking for in the first place has nothing to do with it.

The worst response you can get from your friendly reader is something like this: "Oh, I thought it was very interesting." Forget it, it's all over. If your objective movie reader thinks what you wrote was very interesting, move on. What you do need is this: "Gosh, this was fantastic, great, I loved it." Now you might be in business. The blah opinions and all their justifications will kill you, both emotionally and practically.

Participate in a Writer's Group

If collaboration is not really for you, you may still benefit from participating in a writers' group for screenwriters or a more informal network of friends who are also working on writing screenplays. As you progress through your work, you'll definitely need to bounce your ideas off other people—your potential audiences—and having a supportive group that will give you constructive criticism can be very helpful.

A Critical Approach

There is another and very important advantage to having a well-run writing/reading group. Essentially, you will be forming the classical workshop. Not only is the purpose for you to read your stuff and get objective opinions, it is for you, and all the others, to learn from being a critic yourselves.

To be a good critic you have to concentrate on the work; when you find something that you think needs attention in someone else's work, you are automatically drawn to wonder if you have the same problem in your own writing. So this whole operation works both ways for all. Don't take every little piece of criticism to heart. Take what you need and move on.

Chapter 10

The Screenplay: An Adaptable Creature

Why Write an Adaptation?

It has been estimated that well over half of all feature-length films made since 1920 have been based on plays or novels. This doesn't mean there are few ideas around; more often than not, the reason behind adaptation has been to try and capitalize on the advance success of the forerunner. And yet, the most frequent complaint about book adaptations is, "It wasn't as good as the book."

Adaptation is so popular, there is an Academy Award category for screenplays based on material previously produced or published. Here are a few examples of screenwriters who have won the Oscar in this category:

> 2005: *Brokeback Mountain*, Larry McMurtry and Diana Ossana, based on the short story by E. Annie Proulx.
> 2004: *Sideways*, Alexander Payne and Jim Taylor, based on the book by Rex Picket.
> 2003: *The Lord of the Rings*: *Return of the King*, Fran Walsh and Peter Jackson, based on the book by J. R. R. Tolkien.

2002: *The Pianist*, Ronald Harwood, based on the book by Wladyslaw Szpilman.

2001: *A Beautiful Mind*, Akiva Goldsman, based on the book by Sylvia Nasar.

2000: *Traffic*, Stephen Gaghan, based on 1990 British TV miniseries.

For those who might be serious about adaptations, it would be a good idea to perhaps dig out a couple of original works that became films and compare them to the way in which the adaptations were accomplished. Be warned, there's quite a selection to pick from; about 85 percent of all Oscar-winning best pictures are adaptations. You will probably find that many of the adaptations were successful because the adaptor didn't slavishly follow the original.

Hard Look at Adaptation

You may love the idea of adaptations, but don't write them unless you can get the rites to the material. This might be hard since the material oftentimes belongs to a studio. Studios bank on the sequels of top grossing films. They have already proven their legs at the box office. If you can, get the rites to a small book you love (if it is available) or adapt one of your own books if you have written one.

Don't fool yourself, adaptation does not make everything easier. Whatever you choose to adapt has been created in an entirely different medium, and adapting it for the screen will require you to make changes that may inadvertently affect the intent or quality of the work. Of course, some works are much more easily adapted for the movies. There may be some truth in the assertion that author Michael Crichton writes his books as extended film treatments, thus making them simpler to adapt. Have you read *Jurassic Park*? If so, you may have noticed that it reads just like a movie. However, that's not usually the case with most novels.

Hit Trick

If you were going to work on trying to convert a novel to the screen that was written by a famous contemporary author, you might find working in his or her shadow not only intimidating but also daunting. Adapting the works of authors long dead might be a better bet, except that the really good ones will be in short supply, having already been adapted as films.

Consider the Logistics

You will also need to consider the time period and the set requirements needed for the work you plan to adapt into a screenplay. If the original you are working with deals with a time long past, getting together the set, costumes, and other props make period pieces a much more difficult sale because of the budget. Your best bet would be to keep the same story and turn it into present day, but this is very tricky, and you may be taking on way too much. As far as I am concerned it is tough enough writing a good screenplay so why make it more difficult? But in the end always let your passion lead because this is where your best work will be.

Slippery When Wet: Copyright Issues

The first problem to be solved in adaptation is the issue of copyright. It is not a good idea to write an adaptation in the hope that the owner of the rights is going to be so pleased that he or she will be forever grateful to you—that's wishful thinking. Instead, the owner of the material will probably be talking to a lawyer. Just be forewarned, it is impractical to decide to write an adaptation just because you happen to love the subject matter of an original published work. I had a student who insisted on adapting *The Secret Life of Bees*. She was forewarned. The movie has now been made and she can't even show the script as a sample of her writing.

Writer Beware!

The famous humorist Art Buchwald sent a story outline he had written to Paramount Studios about an African prince who comes to America to find a bride. The written story was copyrighted, but the idea wasn't. Paramount decided to take the idea and make its own movie, **Coming to America**, without giving Buchwald credit. As a result, Buchwald sued Paramount for breach of agreement and won.

The only exception to the rule of getting the rights is if the work you choose to adapt is in the public domain—that is, the copyright has expired and no person or estate holds the rights to the work, or the work was created before copyright laws existed. In this case, you'll be free to adapt the work in any way you like (of course, you'll still need to give credit to the original author). The best examples of works in the public domain quite often adapted for the movies are the plays written by William Shakespeare. Think just how many times his works have been adapted, both successfully and unsuccessfully, for films. In fact, why not rent two or three different productions of the same film and then compare how they were adapted for the screen?

Novels, Short Stories, and Plays

One of the most popular objects of adaptation is the novel. There's plenty of material in a novel to serve as a plot and story of a film. In fact, you are going to have the opposite problem—there'll be a lot of condensing to do. The issue of length is important—remember that you have to aim for a screenplay of about 120 pages.

Putting that to one side, you also have to look at the time frame of the novel you are working with. Does it cover, for instance, a few centuries, or perhaps just forty or fifty years, or even less? A time frame of a generation or more obviously presents aging concerns for the cast and the makeup department.

Bare Necessities

Most novels run to around 125,000 words or thereabouts, which means at least 250 pages and up. Something has to go; the eternal question in the adaptation game is, what? The best way to approach the problem is not to fret about what to cut, but to decide what is essential. This comes down to analyzing exactly what the novel is about and what its purpose is.

Hit Trick

"You don't learn how to write a screenplay by just reading screenplays and watching. It's about developing the kind of mind that sees and makes drama. You can do this in a kind or holistic way by reading history and theology and psychology, reading great fiction and poetry, and plays. You develop an eye for the structures of everything and look for the patterns that help you become a dramatist." —Robin Swicord, am American screenwriter, coproducer, executive producer. Her films include, but are not limited to, **Memoirs of a Geisha, Matilda, Little Women, and The Red Coat.**

Try to identify the major elements in the novel; these should include the protagonist, antagonist, and major secondary characters and their value to the progression of the story. What is the conflict and which chapters/scenes contain conflict development? Look at the structure and mark off the three acts. Go right through the book to the climax. And make sure that you identify the climax and its resolution!

Pay particular attention to the second act. You may remember the points already made about the second act in a film often being the weakest. Well, the same frequently happens in a novel. That being the case, it will be the second act where you might be able to do your finest cutting. Writer and friend, Earl Wallace, who I had the great honor of collaborating with on a screenplay, wrote the longest running miniseries in history, *Winds of War*, and *War and Remembrance*, for Dan Curtis, based on the novels by Herman Wouk. I asked Earl what it's like doing adaptations and he told me it all depends on the quality of the book. With great novels the difficulty is paring them down, with bad novels the only thing that remains is the title!

What to Leave Out

One first step is to reduce the number of characters or perhaps combine two of them into one. It is well-known that in *Gone with the Wind*, which was based on a fairly long book, many characters were either cut altogether or merged into a single one. Try to end up with four strong characters. You will find that the extra characters are often involved in a subplot. Look closely; perhaps the subplot isn't essential to the major point of the story and could be dropped altogether.

Prose and Show

Some novelists are prone to extravagant prose with long descriptions of characters and places. Others seem to love to "tell" the reader what their characters are feeling. Film is an entirely different medium. It is the haiku of writing. I tell students to think of the novelist as the long distance runner and the screenwriter as the acrobat! Read screenplays. Film is the art of less.

Adapting a Short Story

Working with a short story, newspaper article, or another piece of writing of similar length, you've got the opposite problem—the original work may not have sufficient depth and girth to sustain a feature-length film without expansion. That means you are going to have to add on to the work as you adapt it into a script. Sometimes this proves to be so difficult, more than a few studios have bought the rights to a short story only to end up using the title and coming up with an entirely different story for the screenplay. The bulk of the picture becomes the creation of the scriptwriter.

Writer Beware!

Take a look at the 2002 movie, **Adaptation,** directed by Spike Jonze and written by one of the most original screenwriters of our time, Charlie Kaufman. It portrays a lovelorn screenwriter who turns to his less talented twin brother for help when his efforts to adapt a nonfiction book go nowhere.

Adapting a Play

As we all know, plays are usually restricted to interior sets in a theater. This makes them difficult to adapt for the screen. The common device is "opening them out," meaning finding reasons to be on location so that the film version doesn't look like a play caught on film. Flashbacks are often used to give a back story to what wasn't deemed appropriate in the theatrical original. In the theater, reality isn't nearly as paramount as it is in film; therefore, the plays that imply realism often fare better in adaptation.

Some plays can gain immeasurably in film by adding tremendous scope to the restricted play format. The numerous adaptations of Shakespeare's plays serve as a good example of this: *Hamlet* has been adapted eight times, the most impressive of which is considered to be Grigori Kozintsev's 1964 version. Then there is *Henry V* and Laurence Olivier's 1944 production, which demonstrates the one big film advantage with the full staging of the Battle of Agincourt.

"The Book Was Better" Syndrome

Why is it that moviegoers can so often be heard saying these words as they come out of a cinema after watching a film based on a highly successful book: "It wasn't as good as the book." The reason is probably because audiences think the filmmakers just took the book as is and turned it into a film. They don't understand the problems and logistics involved when adapting a work, especially a famous and popular one. There is one good reason for the book/film problem: When people read a book, they bring all that they are to it, everything—their prejudices, hopes, fears, background, the lot. So along comes a move studio and makes a film of "their" book.

Written works have the luxury of spending time giving information, providing emotional feelings to convey motives, and including detailed descriptions of whatever the author wishes to describe. The adaptor has to figure out ways to get the same information to the audience. How dare they cast Tom Cruise without asking, when the reader had visualized the main character as Tom Hanks? The readers form their own interpretations and visualizations of a book, then movie people step on their toes when they do something else in the film.

As Good as the Book

However, there are some adaptations that were successful with the film audiences. *To Kill a Mockingbird* is Harper Lee's only novel, for which she won the 1960 Pulitzer Prize. In fact, librarians across the country have given the book the highest honor by voting it the best novel of the twentieth century. In 1962, the novel was adapted for the screen and became a box-office hit. As a result, the screenwriter who adapted the novel for the screen, Horton Foote, won an Oscar for best screenplay. Other Oscars went to Gregory Peck for best actor and Henry Bumstead and Alexander Golitzen for best art direction. *To Kill a Mockingbird* is a compelling story in both formats. So, combining the talents of the screenwriter, director, etc., allowed for a successful adaptation. Take a look at both the novel and then the film; it's a great example of success.

Chapter 11

Welcome to the Jungle: Hollywood

The Studio

Hollywood has been called a state of mind rather than a place, and there's a strong element of truth to that. But, truly, Hollywood is a generic term that refers to a sort of center where movies are made. However, American movies are actually made all over the place: San Francisco, New York, Toronto, London, Paris, Rome, and elsewhere throughout the world. But wherever they are made, the mentality is the same. And as you already know, wherever the film production is taking place, it can't happen without those 120 three-hole-punched pages—the script.

Scriptwriters in the studios of yesterday came to work in the morning and were paid by the week. In every studio there was a writers' section or wing. If a writer deserved it, he or she was assigned a secretary to type up clean drafts of handwritten or very roughly typed pages. Studio heads always worried that their writers weren't doing enough work; and in some cases, they had a reason for worrying.

Literature and the Movies

Some of the most famous literary names in America spent time in Hollywood, with varying degrees of success. These include Nunnally Johnson, Dudley Nichols, F. Scott Fitzgerald, William Faulkner, Nathanael West, and Aldous Huxley. As it turned out, not all the big-name literary writers could write screenplays. It's also fair to say that few of the established screenwriters had any success writing novels.

This would seem to confirm that literary talent is not a necessary ingredient for a scriptwriter to have. What is absolutely necessary is visual imagination together with the knowledge of how movies work and how a film is put together. There are many stories about literary luminaries arriving in Hollywood expecting to polish off a screenplay in a few days. In part, this attitude was the result of disdain the rest of society held for the filmmaking industry.

The Majors

Hollywood emerged into the film scene relatively early; by the 1930s, it ruled the cinematic landscape, and yet it was made up of only a few big studios on the West Coast. These studios soon became known as the majors, and they included the following giants:

- Buena Vista
- Fox
- Metro-Goldwyn-Mayer (MGM)
- Paramount
- Sony
- Warner Bros.
- Twentieth Century Fox

Each studio had vast lots that housed their production stages, sound recording, music, cinematographers, technical departments, and crew—in short, everything that was required to make movies on site. They also owned the cinemas that screened the movies they produced.

The Players

In Hollywood it's a good thing to have clout, even though it may not last forever. The upper-echelon players, almost always based on the revenues they pull in, make decisions. The prized position is to be able to "green light" a script, that means giving it the go ahead to be made.

Hit Trick

"You've got to know somebody who knows somebody and you've got to be here. You can't do it from out of town. If you want to be in movies, in the business, you've got to be in L.A. I mean I'm not here because I love it here." —Jim Kouf, an American screenwriter, director, and producer. His movies include, but are not limited to, **Stakeout**, **Rushhour**, **Snow Dogs**, and **Gang Relater**.

It's interesting for many years I lived out of town and I think it did hurt my career, but in many ways it soothed my soul. I raised my daughter in the small town of Pacific Grove known as "Butterfly Town, USA." I'd have to drive seven hours to get to a meeting and it was tough. Now I am back in beautiful downtown Burbank. It is more convenient, I no longer have excuses for not networking and I have made much better contacts. But you don't have to move here to write. You can write an arsenal of screenplays anywhere in the world. Wait until you sell something, or have an agent, or a very good reason to move before you pack up.

When a business is full of beautiful and talented people who earn immense sums of money, it's not hard to see why they wield so much power. The "A List," referred to so many times, leads to many good things: exposure, party invitations, free catered meals, and so on. But whether stars, or studio execs, or producers, they are an elite handful.

The Front Office

The front office is where most of the big studio decisions are made, except, that is, from wherever the most chic watering hole in Beverly Hills happens to be at the time you are in town. If you manage to make your way into a front office, it's best to be accompanied by an agent or a lawyer. When you are up against those smooth and very persuasive Hollywood executives, it makes very good sense to have professional advice by your side. What you are also going to be dealing with is personality, yours and the other guy's. You should understand that a lot of money could be made in the movie business, even if you don't have any talent. Sure, you can rely on your talent, but you also need the business smarts to make it through the negotiation process.

Writer Beware!

Rent a copy of Robert Altman's **The Player** (1992). Apart from being a highly entertaining picture with about sixty cameo appearances by Hollywood stars, it has a sharp satirical edge to it (Altman's signature). **The Player** is pretty close to the way things really are in Hollywood and provides insight into the way the industry works.

This is true of any business, of course, but remember that the movie business is even tenser because the stakes are higher. There are very few businesses where even a novice has the possibility, just on the nod of one person, to make upwards of $100,000 on the delivery of 120 typed pages that constitute a film script.

Trying to Circumvent the System

If you happen to be the author of a spec script in production and you live in the middle of Ohio and do not have a heavy-hitting Hollywood agent, the best thing to be done is to hope they spell your name right on the credits and get on with the next spec script. However, if you are an ace schmoozer living on the outskirts, or even the in-skirts, of Malibu, things could be different. There is no getting around it. Networking is everything.

The Budget

As the studio signs up a film project, it is allotted a specific budget. The budget has many functions; one, obviously, is to slot expenditures into their appropriate categories. A major demarcation line that separates the expenditures is whether they are made before or during film production (when the film is being shot). The difference between these two types of expenditures is referred to as "above or below the line." (As it happens, film people are also referred to as being above or below the line.)

Expenses above the line are made prior to the shooting process, and one of these expenses is purchasing the screenplay—that's where you come in. Also included are the producers, director, stars, and other actors. If you want to generalize, "above the line" folks are all those who come before or immediately under the opening credits.

Below the line are the people who make the picture: the cinematographer, editor, assistant director, production assistant, and so on. They come after the opening credits, frequently running at the end of the picture, which nowadays is still doing its thing when audiences have fled the cinema. Caterers and car services are often on the list as well. Unfortunately, much of the prestige is lost in this day and age.

Film Unions

The major studios are union signatories, which means they use only union talent and pay union wages; this adds about 30 percent to the budget. You don't need to be an accountant to work out how much this can add to the finished budget of a production. When the costs of promotion and distribution are factored in, it becomes very clear why a movie from plain paper all the way to silver screen can cost $40 million and change.

The independent film companies may not be union signatories, which can help them to make do with lower budgets. The financing of indie pictures comes from a wide variety of sources: network and cable, foreign exhibitors and distributors, and private investors. To give you an estimate, I just finished producing my first movie, *Surviving Eden*, starring Cheri Oteri, Peter Dinklage, Jane Lynch, and John Landis. We made it on a million dollar budget. That's because unions allowed deferments on some wages and there are tax incentives for filming in various regions. Financing a film can be almost as creative • as writing one.

Your Place in This World

The most difficult thing to accomplish is to create what is original. Anyone can adapt, change, or copy. In the film business they do it all the time, and even take credit for it. Writers in Hollywood work very hard on creating and polishing, putting the right words and stories together, yet many of them don't get the credit they deserve. Unfortunately, it must be said that the Hollywood industry doesn't hold screenwriters in great esteem.

Often, writers are taken for granted and their work is seen as something to work with, not a finished product. The opinion in Hollywood is that scriptwriters don't have much in the way of clout (the exception is if you are an Oscar winner), and so writers are pretty low on the prestige totem pole. Many of the people who can't write—agents, directors, actors, reviewers, and executives—will insist on putting their two cents in, invited or not. To repeat the adage: Every cabdriver in Los Angeles has a script in progress. But this shouldn't discourage your efforts. Screenwriting can be a fulfilling endeavor, as long as you know what to expect.

A Difficult Business

The status of the writer in Hollywood probably hasn't changed very much over the years. When Hollywood writers do gain prestige, it's usually when they decide to direct their own films. In fairness, the nature of the business where many people can have input to a picture doesn't help much. Another factor is the amount of money at stake.

For example, the reputation of a film executive rests on the success of a film he or she personally gave the green light to, and the project receives a budget of $10 million. The temptation to interfere must be immense—who could stand by and watch the process that will make or break your career?

Adding to the conflict of interest is the position of the director, who is responsible for the artistic as well as commercial success of the film. If the film's a failure, who knows if the director will ever get another project to work on. The pressures are there, and sometimes the players can't all agree on what's best. Unfortunately, the screenwriter is left out of these struggles. Once the studio purchases the script, it's pretty much out of the screenwriter's hands.

Writer Beware!

All writers should rejoice in the fact that they originate—that's the difficult part; copying is a cinch. Nevertheless, the price is often that rejection will come, and many times it is justified. The minute you create and put what you create out there to be judged, you are open to criticism and disagreement.

The Director and the Screenwriter

If mutual respect exists between the writer and the director—and it often does—then the production will benefit. A good working relationship is generally a result of working together. It may even happen if the writer is on his or her first script and the director is an old hand at the game. In this case, the director may act as the writer's mentor.

However, be aware that there have been endless tales about the horrendous rows and shouting matches between writers and directors. It seems to be in the nature of the craft that the creative egos of the two are designed to clash. The problems stem from the number of opinions that get involved in the production. For instance, a writer will do a rewrite of scene 235 for the shooting schedule. He hands it to the director the night before the shooting. The director takes it to his home in Beverly Hills and on the way there shows it to the driver of the studio limo. When he gets home he shows the scene to his wife.

After a couple of cocktails before dinner, the director puts in a call to the writer, who takes it on the cellular phone in his car on his way home to Tarzana in the Valley. The director tells the writer in short order that the scene will have to be redone, it's just not what he wants. What he neglects to mention to the writer is that he hasn't actually read the scene himself.

Dealing with Envy

Another part of the problem is the unexpressed, sublimated envy of the writer in the industry. After all, the writer is the only one who originates new material. To acknowledge that the picture you are working on is not really yours, but has been written by someone else, is difficult to stomach for many people. As some screenwriters have suggested, perhaps the reason they aren't allowed on the set is that people don't want to be reminded that the film was the screenwriter's idea.

Who Wrote It?

It has always been the nature of the writing game that readers will praise a book, be really enthusiastic about it, but not know the name of the author. This is much the same in the movie industry—and perhaps even more so. When you've got a book, the author's name is right there on the cover. But when you rent a video or buy a DVD, the screenwriter's name is hidden in the credits. Film fans often remember the name of the director, but they rarely know who wrote the screenplay.

Hit Trick

"It isn't what happens to people on a page-it's what happens to a reader in his heart and mind." —Gordon Lish, an author, editor, and teacher.

In a sense, this is because the screenwriter writes for the industry. By the time the film is made, it has been worked on by so many people that the script itself has taken a backseat to the actual movie, complete with actors, scenes, and dialogue. That's why the only time a screenwriter gets visibility is on Oscar night, and then there are only two of them up at the podium.

The Best-Known Scriptwriters

The two most visible screenwriters are probably William Goldman and Robert Towne. Goldman wrote *Butch Cassidy and the Sundance Kid* (1969), *The Stepford Wives* (1975), *Marathon Man* (1976), and *All the President's Men* (1976). These were the most successful among many other screenplays and books. He also contributed additional unaccredited work to many films as a script doctor. One of the reasons for William Goldman's celebrity, apart from the films he's scripted, is a book he published in 1983 called *Adventures in the Screen Trade: A Personal View of Hollywood and Screenwriting*. It has become more or less required reading for budding screenwriters.

Towne wrote *Bonnie & Clyde* (1967), *Chinatown* (1974), and many other films, both credited and unaccredited. It's interesting to note that in 1997 Robert Towne was presented with the Writers Guild of America's Screen Laurel Award, the WGA's highest award in recognition of his body of work. Some other recipients have been Ruth Prawer Jhabvala, of *Le Divorce* and *The Golden Bowl,* Waldo Salt, of *Coming Home* and *The Day of the Locust,* Woody Allen, of *Scoop* and *Match Point,* Neil Simon, of *The Goodbye Girl* and *The Out of Towners,* and Billy Wilder, of *Sabrina* and *Witness for the Prosecution.* The more recent recipients include Betty Comden and Adolph Green (2001).

And who can forget two of the films they wrote, *Singin' in the Rain* and *The Band Wagon*, even if the names of the scriptwriters can't be remembered?

Your Screenplay's Place: The MPAA System

The Motion Picture Association of America (MPAA) administers a rating system of content for each film submitted to its board. The film producer makes the submission; although submission is voluntary, most producers do go along with the board's decision, because without a rating the chances of a good distribution deal are slight. If there is disagreement, the director or distributor can appeal a particular rating. The board reviews the film as appealed and makes its final decision.

It would be good for you to be aware of each rating, what it represents, and the audience that is affected by the rating. The following are the MPAA ratings.

> **G:** General Audiences—All Ages Admitted. Although the "G" rating doesn't necessarily signal a children's film, it does indicate that there is nothing in the picture that, in the opinion of the MPAA rating board, would be offensive to virtually anyone in terms of language, nudity, sex, and violence.
>
> **PG:** Parental Guidance Suggested. Some Material May Not Be Suitable for Children. The rating indicates that parents need to inquire about the film before they let their children attend. While there may be nothing offensive in the film, the content may simply not be appropriate for young children.
>
> **PG-13:** Parents Strongly Cautioned. Some Material May Be Inappropriate for Children Under 13. A sterner warning for parents, alerting them to be very careful about letting their preteen children attend a viewing.

R: Restricted. Under 17 Requires Accompanying Parent or Adult Guardian. This indicates that some adult material is contained in the film and that parents are strongly urged to find out if they think it is suitable for their children to accompany them.

NC-17: No One 17 and Under Admitted. The rating doesn't mean the film is obscene or pornographic—these are legal terms, so the board does not use them. However, if a film does contain excessive violence, graphic sexual content, or drug abuse, the board may rate it NC-17, which takes away the parents' choice to allow or prohibit their children from watching the film. Few mainstream films merit this rating, perhaps because most cinemas choose not to screen these movies.

Producers generally know what rating they are aiming for even before film production begins, and it may benefit you to keep this information in mind, too, as you are working on and marketing your script.

Chapter 12

Try Going "Alternative"

The Independent Studio

Making a top-grossing film is not the only target to aim for, nor is working with the major studios, of which there are currently only seven. And the way the movie-making business changes, that number may not be accurate by the time this book is on the stacks.

Independent films, or indies, are different from the big-league movies. Independent studios may not be union signatories, their budgets are generally lower, and their financing comes from a variety of sources. (In the case of the major film studios, the money comes from the bank.) For a variety of reasons it is believed that the newer screenwriter is more apt to sell to an indie studio than to a major one.

The spectrum of indie productions goes all the way from those who have strong distribution connections with the majors to those who have to beg, borrow, and scavenge for money to rent equipment and buy film stock. The philosophy of the indie production unit can be just as diverse and often the audiences are very seriously motivated moviegoers. Indie productions cover a wide variety of minority-based productions: gay, lesbian, and a vast ethnic and political diversity.

Independent Producers

Independent producers have become a major force in the movie-production industry. The typical image of an indie producer is of a person strapped for cash who has to charge the last of his or her quickly diminishing production budget on a credit card. However, as many have become more successful, they enter bigger stakes, working for what are known as the minimajor studios; often, the major studios distribute their products domestically. These movies tend to leave the PG-13 mold of the basic audience-pleasing kind of movie, and so they are known to be more artistic than commercial.

Artistic Visionaries

Indie producers and directors frequently are without the concern for profit that the major studios seek. Their credo tends to be the preservation of artistic integrity. Here are some of the better-known indie-minded filmmakers: Orson Welles, Sam Fuller, John Cassavetes, Ed Wood, and Radley Metzger.

The indie productions don't go unnoticed by Hollywood; Robert Redford's Sundance Festival in Utah has grown to be a virtual force as a showcase for independent producers. It draws players from the majors and includes films from around the world. While there are other indie festivals, it's probably fair to say that Sundance has upped the energy of the independent filmmaker.

The Sundance Institute

The Institute supports the development and emergence of screenwriters and directors. Redford has said that over the past fifteen years there has been a noticeable change in the quality and sophistication of scriptwriting. Redford also said that in the Sundance Screenwriters Lab the focus is on the development of screenwriting because of the current poor scripts.

An attitude not prevalent in Hollywood that comes from Redford is his respect for screenwriters. He had the writers of *Quiz Show* and *A River Runs Through It* involved, even though they were not required to do rewrites. Redford is on record as saying that he doesn't believe writers should feel like distant cousins to a project when they turn their scripts in.

The Stigma of an Art Label

The commercial/art argument has been with us for decades, of course. Another way to describe it is to say that what is popular is commercial and what is not is artistic, the implication being that people of lesser intellectual ability like what's popular.

As far as motion pictures are concerned, the same set of values apply, even within the industry, where it might be read in the trade press that a certain new film was an art house release. To the money people in Hollywood, getting the label "art" on a picture is a financial death prediction, although sometimes they are pleasantly surprised.

Writer Beware!

If writers get involved with underfinanced independent producers, they should seek legal advice, particularly if they don't have an agent. Most indie producers today ask for free options. This means the producer has a fixed time, six months to a year, to shop the project around in an effort to raise finance.

When so much money is at risk (most people could live a very comfortable life on the production budget of the average film), it's not surprising that the financial czars of the studios take a hard line when it comes to the subject matter of a proposed film. This has led to a jumping on the bandwagon kind of mentality. In other words, if "boy" films are hot and suddenly making lots of money, then a studio chief might decree the green light to anything similar and hope it does as well. This follow-the-leader way of doing things, which is frequently the butt of cynical criticism from commentators, is the direct result of trying to minimize something called "investment risk management."

Today, Hollywood remains disinclined to take risks because of rising production costs, which everyone complains about but nobody seems to do anything about. The trends established in the late 1980s continue with sequels and blockbusters. Thus there is room for the independents, who with their lower production costs, can and do take risks.

It Can Work

A few years ago a group of completely unknown independent filmmakers got together to make a film; they managed to raise a budget of around $60,000. The picture did not have any of the polish of a major studio production, but then, it didn't cost quite the same to make. However, mainly through word of mouth, it built an audience. The box-office receipts have been said to total in the region of $140 million; the film was called *The Blair Witch Project.*

Writer Beware!

The Ultra-Low-Budget movie began to gain acceptance in the early 1990s when three features achieved success at film festivals. This led to their producers finding theatrical distributors. The films were Nick Gomez's **Laws of Gravity**, Gregg Araki's **The Living End**, and Robert Rodriguez's **El Mariachi**. The budgets for these pictures ranged from $7,225 to $38,000.

Because of the economics of film production, European companies have been mounting coproductions. It is estimated that 150 films were made in France in the early 2000s using this type of financing. As the exhibition markets expand into new avenues, the need for a greater number of films (product) is rising. This, of course, means the need for a greater number of good scripts should follow.

Neophyte screenwriters should look beyond the traditional means of film production. While it may not be the safest way to go, provided a writer has good advice, there is every reason to presume that the outcome can be successful. Writers should not overlook the market if for no other reason than that the working environment is going to be far different from that of the majors.

Go Ahead and Get Shorty

Some people initially look at the short film in the same way that others look at the short story. Because one is shorter than a feature film and the other shorter than a novel, they must both be easier to produce and write. Not quite. The difference between them is not just a question of length. In modern film it is the subject matter and market that tends to dictate the length of the film; in a short story the restriction is generally on the time and place of the action, as well as the number of characters and the depth of character development.

Types of Short Films

The Academy of Motion Picture Arts and Sciences, the outfit that gives out the Oscars, has a set of rules governing the definitions of acceptable product. Rule 19 covers special rules for the short film awards. The definition and categories are as follows:

1. A short film is defined as a motion picture that is not more than forty minutes in running time (including all credits).

2. An award shall be given for the best achievement in each of two categories:

   1. **Animated Films.** An animated film usually falls into one of the two general fields of animation: character or abstract. Some of the techniques of animating films include cel animation, computer animation, stop-motion, clay animation, puppets, pixilation, cutouts, pins, camera multiple pass imagery, kaleidoscopic effects, and drawing on the film frame itself.

2.   **Live Action Films.** A live action film utilizes primarily live action techniques as the basic medium of entertainment.

The definition goes on to say that documentary shorts will not be accepted in either category. It also states that previews and advertising films shall be excluded.

The Documentary

At first glance it might seem odd that documentary films would need a screenwriter. Most people probably think that some bearded person, with a movie camera clutched in his hands, turns the lens toward a homeless person in the gutter and films away. It's not quite like that; if it were, it might be said that the person who turned his video camera on Rodney King was a documentary filmmaker.

The old saying about the computer, "garbage in, garbage out," applies equally to the documentary film. The very title, documentary, would indicate that it is a visual record of a factual set of occurrences. However, just like written reporting, much has to do with the degree of selection and/or omission.

The definition set by the Academy of Motion Picture Arts and Sciences reads:

1.   A documentary film is defined as a nonfiction motion picture dealing creatively with cultural, artistic, historical, social, economic, or other subjects. It may be photographed in actual occurrence, or may employ partial re-enactment, stock footage, still, animation, stop-motion, or other techniques, as long as the emphasis is on factual content and not on fiction.

The two categories into which the documentary awards are divided are:

Documentary Feature: films more than forty minutes running time.

Documentary Short Subject: films forty minutes or fewer (including all credits) in running time.

2. A film considered to be primarily a promotional film, a purely technical instructional film, or an essentially unfiltered record of a performance will not be considered eligible as a documentary.

Who? The Market

The eventual market for the completed production will depend to a certain extent on its financial backing. Is it a commercially sponsored film? Did the producer get the green light by a PBS station? Is there a distributor involved? Will the picture be entered into the various film festivals around the country?

Unless the writer is part of the production segment of the film, obviously his or her involvement is going to be minimal and limited to the purpose of the production. A great many documentary productions are made out of an intense emotional angst about the subject; for instance, the homeless and the starving. On the other hand, many are made by film school graduates anxious to put their education to work.

The Motive-ation

The attitude and motivation of the reporter/film person can very often, if he or she is not scrupulously alert, be subverted because of a serious need to prove a predetermined point. Thus, only that which supports the argument is given value, what doesn't is left out—omitted. It is because of this penchant in us all that drug researchers developed the double-blind system where neither the subject nor the dispenser knows who is getting what—the placebo or the real thing.

Hit Trick

"I do whatever research I need as late as possible because I don't like to interfere with the creative flow . . . . I don't want to stop in the middle of an emotional scene and have to go to the library." —Steven DeSouza, a screenwriter. His films include, but are not limited to, **The Ghost Who Walks**, **Return of the Ninja**, **Isobar**, **Street Fighter**, **Knock Off**, **Judge Dredd**, **Beverly Hills Cop III**, and **The Flintstones.**

While sometimes something just happens without planning, that is not how you should go about writing and making a documentary. By all means take advantage of unplanned events, but don't count on them happening just when you'd like them to. If it is at all possible, do as much research as is practical.

As the writer of the production you should have a working knowledge of what equipment is going to be used on the shoot. Get to know the crew; it's probably going to be a compact one, which makes it all the more important that you work well together.

Preparing the Script

A lot will depend on how it came about that you are working on the script. Is the producer/director a friend? Were you hired because you're something of an expert in the subject of the film? Did you pitch the idea to the producer? Is your father putting up the money? Whatever the reason, it is essential that you involve yourself absolutely in the subject matter and purpose of the project.

If it is at all possible, it would be an excellent idea for you to work or be associated with the subject of the film. Obviously, this isn't always going to be possible. But say, for instance, the film is intended to be a documentary on the differences between New York City and London cabs. Naturally, you can do all the background research from the available records.

Then you should try to be taken on as a driver or, at least, a backup person in the office of the cab company in both cities, and that should include whatever vehicle service facilities they have. Get to know the cabbies, get to know the complaints, get to know the customers. By the time your research is finished you should be a good candidate for a permanent job. (It might come in useful while you're waiting for your next script assignment.)

Script Format

What will be required from the scriptwriter will depend on the type of documentary production. If it is set up to cover an event, say the track test for a new racing car, then the structure will tend to be predetermined. The writer will initially probably be limited to preparing a shot list, establishing shots, preparation of the vehicle shots, and so on. He or she will then get involved in viewing the shooting, rushes, and the rough-cut edits.

Then it will be back to the keyboard to produce a narration script. By that time the writer should have a very good idea of what needs to be the accompanying audio to run over the visual shots. For example, the shot may be of the driver about to do some difficult technical maneuver. The narration might prime the audience on what the driver is going to try to accomplish.

IDA—Not Your Grandmother in Iowa

The International Documentary Association is a nonprofit organization that has been around since 1982. Its purpose is to support nonfiction and video makers. If you intend to become a documentary film or video maker, it's just about essential that you get involved with the IDA. It has a tremendous resource capability, including in-depth information about submitting grant proposals to a seemingly endless list of national and international festivals. And it also offers what is called the IDA fiscal sponsorship, which means IDA will act as an overseer of progress of your production and as a distributor of funds.

Of course, to get access to any of these programs you have to become a member. Information about membership is available by phone at(213) 534-3600 or by mail, at 1201 West 5th Street, Suite M320, Los Angeles, CA 90017-1461. Membership fee includes subscription to the International Documentary Magazine (ten issues per year), and full-time student membership discounts are available as well.

The membership of the association includes people from across the production spectrum: producers, directors, writers, editors, technicians, and members of the public. To get more information, go to their Web site at *www.documentary.org*.

You, a Teacher?

The increased use of video often makes it difficult for the nonprofessional to distinguish between film and video, and in many ways it doesn't make a tremendous amount of difference to the scriptwriter. The technical debate on the comparable attributes of the two mediums takes on less importance in situations where the audience reception isn't crucial. This doesn't mean to say that second-best will do, only that the purpose of the production is not designed to reach the high technical standards of, say, *Saving Private Ryan*.

The power of film and video educational programs has proved their worth. A lecture that incorporates the study of a scientific instrument that would be impossible for students to see in an auditorium becomes simple when the instrument can be viewed either in the classroom or in the school audiovisual library, with a voice-over by the professor.

The kind of educational program that presents the greatest test of skill to the scriptwriter is one in which the information is delivered by an academic. The ditch that can easily be fallen into is the dreaded "talking heads"—two people, one delivering a message to the other, are photographed. One is showing how to do something, while the other person is photographed listening, and sometimes reacting, to what has been said. When edited together, the result is two talking heads talking and listening to each other.

"Talking heads" are the backbone of television talk shows and news broadcasts, where at least there is usually the option of cutting away to live action. The results are generally boring in direct relationship to the amount of live action included in the segment. A prescripted educational program has an advantage that the talk-show program generally lacks: time.

Simple But Good

Here is an actual program example: A bank wants a series of programs that demonstrate to their lenders what a client looks for in a lender (the business of banks is lending money). By the time the professional scriptwriter has been hired the format has been decided upon: The bank expert will be on camera interviewing the client. Immediately, the scriptwriter sees the potential for a boring "talking heads" series of programs.

The scriptwriter proposes that each client be interviewed on the site of her or his business. The scriptwriter will script what will become a series of "cutaways" in which the client, on his or her own, will be involved. The shots will show the client at work; in one case a cattleman in Montana will be shown on horseback, out in the prairie, inspecting his cattle. The question-and-answer segments will then be laid over the visuals as voice-overs.

The result was interest from the audience because they became involved in the client's business. Not exactly complicated—in fact very simple—but the technique altered what could have been a very dry program into one that was quite the opposite. It can be seen from this example why television networks strive so hard to hire personalities their audiences find attractive; something or somebody has to balance out the "talking heads."

Your Baby

The idea of making your own film can be intoxicating. It is presumed that you have spent all the time necessary to learn the practicalities of filmmaking. You know what the camera is capable of doing and you know how important editing will be to the final product. Perhaps you have practiced with a low-cost video camera, which has given you the feel for recorded images.

You should have immersed yourself in indie films and read all the literature you could get hold of. You have been on the Internet, joined indie chat groups, and subscribed to message boards. In other words, the obsession that filmmakers should have has immersed you. Now you feel ready to embark upon one of the most exciting projects in your life: you are to become an independent filmmaker.

At this point you have probably become fixated on the subject of your film. It is something you feel very deeply about; you want to make some kind of statement about it. This is essential because the enthusiasm that comes with these feelings will serve to buoy you over the rough spots ahead. Unless you are independently wealthy or have a sponsor waiting in the wings, your first step will have to be finding the money to make the film.

Finding the Finance

Step number one is writing a proposal, which is really very close to a business plan. The purpose is to present to the potential backer what the film is going to be about. What you will be writing here is a selling document, so it should be couched in business terms. Try to keep any artistic flavor to a minimum; people or companies with money are often wary about the artistic.

Writer Beware!

The one advantage of raising the money to make a documentary is that is easier to explain a documentary than a theatrical picture. Nonfiction films can be qualified and quantified; theatrical pictures are subjective and thus more difficult to explain. They also involve personal preferences.

Keep in mind the adage, "What's in it for me?" Why should they put up the money, and what will they get from it? Perhaps the prestige of backing something they consider socially worthwhile would suit their philosophy. Some organizations have a standard package that they require be completed. Be absolutely sure that you include the type of credit you propose the backers will have on the film.

The best proposals are short, easy to read, and to the point.

Do not ramble on—make every word count. Say why your project is needed and how it will meet that need. Outline the direct and indirect benefits to the sponsors. Cover the production, the members of the crew, and their achievements. If appropriate, include résumés in the package.

The Budget

An essential item will be the budget; the backers need to know how their money is going to be spent, which is not an unreasonable request. There are a number of factors, such as the following, you should have in place before the budget is even calculated:

- How big a crew will you need?
- Will the production be union or nonunion? (Nonunion will produce a much lower budget.)
- Who owns the equipment you'll need? (If you are using your own, then you don't need to include rental costs.)

If the production is going to be a sizable one, then it would pay you to use the services of an experienced production manager. You will probably have to pay the fee for the manager out of your own funds to aid in the proposal. However, if the production is going to be complicated, it would be prudent to have a production manager onboard and therefore part of the budget.

Accuracy

It should go without saying that it is essential that your budget be accurate; don't underestimate it with the idea that the less money requested, the more likely you'll be approved. That's a very short-sighted policy, which could easily result in worrying endlessly all during production that you are going over budget, and where does the shortfall come from?

In most cases your proposal, including the budget, will become part of the legal agreement between you and the backers. Included in the proposal should be estimates of the production time frame: How long will the film take to make? Again, don't fool yourself by giving a short time frame, which could lead to telephone calls and e-mails asking when the picture is going to be finished. The same problems that can beset a big theatrical production, overbudget and overtime, could strike your production, too.

A Treatment

In just the same way as you would write a treatment for a theatrical film pitch, so you need one for an independent picture, irrespective of subject matter. The treatment must be part of your proposal. Keep in mind that it will, not only outline what your production is about and is going to accomplish, but will be a blueprint against which your budget will be referred.

For example, if you intend traveling with your production crew 100 miles upstate, your treatment will cover the necessity for filming an aged, disabled character you need to interview. The budget for that film about cabs in New York City and London would obviously have to include travel expenses. The treatment would cover the reason and purpose for the location travel.

Chapter 13

Writing for Television

Television: A Different Breed

Some people presume that writing for movies and television is pretty much the same, but it's not quite that simple. Some writers are much better at writing for television, while others succeed writing for film. To find out which one you are best suited for will take perseverance. This chapter will explore the area of writing for television.

A Look Back

In 1927 the first television program was transmitted by wire from Washington, D.C., to New York City. Four years later, NBC got into the business and by 1939, it became the first broadcaster to use telephone lines to relay television signals. From that point on, television was off and running.

The 1950s were a pivotal period for the television industry as CBS and ABC joined NBC in competing for viewers. The number of viewers set the advertising rates—the more viewers, the greater the fee charged for advertising time, a concept that hasn't changed (with the exception of paid cable channels and public television stations). But back then, a single company could sponsor an entire program, so you had shows like *The Colgate Comedy Hour with Donald O'Connor* and the *U.S. Steel Hour*.

The Golden Age

At first a novelty, television soon became the current wonder. Audiences would crowd around television sets at specified times in the evenings to watch comic artists such as Milton Berle and Ernie Kovacs. During the same period, color was introduced. Just as importantly, the creative aspects of television underwent a revolution. The period, the 1950s and 1960s, has become known as the Golden Age of Television.

Programs like *The Ed Sullivan Show, This Is Your Life, Lassie, Sgt. Bilko with Phil Silvers,* and *Playhouse 90*, culminating toward the end of the 1950s with *Rod Serling's The Twilight Zone,* caught the imagination of audiences all over the country. Television suddenly became a major threat to the movie business. There was no need to go out for entertainment—it was right there, in your own living room.

A contributing factor to the freedom and standards of television arose from the economics of production. Television programs were relatively inexpensive to produce: A half-hour series might only be a quarter of the cost of a film. Then, too, there were the physical limitations of the television screen, which was not geared to lavish, expansive scenes and vistas. As often happens, restrictions gave creativity a chance, and television was becoming more and more popular, drawing in viewers who would tune in each week to see what would happen to the characters of their favorite show.

Writer Beware!

The Public Broadcasting Service (PBS) was founded in 1969. It is governed by a board of directors made up of broadcasting professionals as well as other citizens. PBS is a private, nonprofit American corporation whose members are the public television stations of the United States and other allied territories. PBS itself does not produce programming; that's done by its member stations.

The Cable Channels

The advent of HBO with its uncut, advertisement-free movies changed the way the studios and producers constructed their financial projections; television had become a source of revenue. Independent producers suddenly had another pool of income to dip into and the data showed that independent movies drew large audiences, particularly in the eighteen- to thirty-four-year-old age groups advertisers wanted to reach; the market was expanding all around.

It wasn't long until the television industry was contracting with Hollywood to make movies exclusively for them. The made-for-television films cost the networks far less to finance than it cost them to rent Hollywood blockbusters. Television could offer a much larger audience at one screening than Hollywood could ever match. Even actors had to consider the visibility television offered over the established movie release.

The expansion in the number of channels available on cable will, in the long run, increase the amount of product needed to feed their audiences. This, in turn, increases the market potential for writers. Today's writers have to be continually aware of the expanding possibilities for their talents and services. Many of the cable channels are and will be genre oriented; as it stands, the outlook for writers appears, for a change, as if it will expand.

Television Writers

Unlike the motion-picture industry, in the early days of television the writer was recognized as a talent and respected as such. The creative centers and production hubs were then based in New York and the writers came from the local areas. Often they were playwrights and radio dramatists. The written word was a major force in the early creative drive of television.

But as the television networks and their affiliate stations expanded throughout the country and gained popularity and financial success, a rift occurred between the creative and the business side.

As the potential for profitability grew, so did the ownership of television companies and its allied forces. The conglomerate fever spread to the point where a company—AOL Time Warner being a prime example—might own an immense worldwide collection of entertainment companies.

Why Do It?

In a nutshell, the advantages held out by writing for television are simple—money and more of it. If that happens to be your main ambition in life as a writer, then in many ways writing for television will simplify your approach to achieving it. There are writers who want to make a difference, to comment in-depth on the human condition; that might mean running into some difficulties.

The fee for a single network half-hour prime-time drama pilot script can range from the Writers Guild scale minimum of $28,687.50 to $250,000 for established writers. While that may sound absolutely wonderful, and it is, it may be the only income you receive for a few years of going through endless rejections. As each year goes by without another sale, the amortized annual income gets more and more stretched, until you might have been better off learning plumbing as a trade.

If you did something similar in the film industry as a drama pilot script for television, and were paid the WGA Theatrical and Television Basic Agreement rates, this is what you might receive: Original Screenplay, Including Treatment: $48,731 to $91,408. Of course, all sorts of conditions and events can bump those figures out of the ballpark. Nevertheless, it can be seen why many writers are now gravitating to television in its various forms.

The Wonder of It All

There's another great benefit to writing for television. One of the most wonderful aspects about it is the feeling you get from knowing how many people have sat in their living rooms watching what you wrote. Not only that, but you have the knowledge of how many professionals in television have approved of what you have written as it passed along the line and was green-lighted for production. Then there are all those actors who have spoken your words with such conviction and emotion. The bulk of my work has been in television.

Hit Trick

"Imagination is being able to think of things that haven't appeared on TV yet." —Henry Beard, American humorist, cofounder of **National Lampoon** magazine.

I am now writing features. Television spoiled me because I got to see my work completed and on the air. In TV when they buy or put you into development the material is almost always filmed. I have sold some features and have lived off the income, but they were never made.

Educate Yourself about Television

Never overlook the prep work you should be doing. It's amazing the number of producers who have reported how many of the spec scripts sent in look as if the writer had only read the TV Guide description.

Try a different analysis tack, this one based on the dramatic content of a program. Pick a top running television show that's in reruns so that a segment is on every day. *Murder, She Wrote* would be a good one because its dramatic structure is so consistent. You will note that the major characters are always the same. They all talk in the same way, dress the same, and have the same habits.

Take a Stab at It: The Structure

Most television writing is done for shows and series that have a set cast of characters, so instead of developing entirely new stories, you have to come up with new ideas for the same basic concept. When it comes to writing for sitcoms and/or a series, a new writer doesn't fix what isn't broken, unless it happens that a major character leaves the show for some reason and a replacement has to be created.

The television writer has to structure the story around commercial breaks, which means that for sitcoms there may be a two-act structure and for a television movie, one of a series, perhaps a seven-act structure. The budding television scriptwriter is urged to watch and analyze a variety of programs, from sitcoms to high drama. Pay particular attention to the structure of each because that is what you will be expected to write to.

Come up with an answer for each type of program you are researching, and pay attention to the following factors:

- Length (in minutes)
- Number of commercial breaks
- How long each commercial break lasts

Breakdown of Acts

The number of commercial breaks will give you the ballpark for number of acts. Of course, the length of the breaks for commercials can be expanded or retracted, depending on the station and time of exhibition. An episodic comedy is about thirty minutes long and consists of two acts. It has a teaser and a tag. Generally the length is twenty-six pages if on film, forty-two if shot on tape.

The number of acts in a structure is relative to the kind of program. It is also relative to whether the program is initially for the networks or cable—commercials or not. Obviously, you would know in advance what kind of program you are aiming to do. Or, if you're lucky, you've been hired to write and know in advance.

The TV Script

Scripts for television vary in layout; part of this is because some programs are taped, others are shot on film. If you are inclined to have a go at the episodic or situation comedy segments of the television arena, you should understand that the executives will be looking for network-approved writers; they go with what they know. This is particularly so if the show is a new one; they have enough to worry about without testing the waters with fresh writing talent. But once the show has become established, the situation changes.

For established shows and series, the script layout is very close to the one used in a spec script for movies. At the beginning of your script, just as in a film script, start by typing FADE IN. It's usually the form to follow that with the teaser (see following section) and then break to a new page, which is titled ACT ONE (at center top). Some production outfits like their writers to type END OF ACT ONE about three spaces after the actual end of the act. You would then go to a new page and repeat the opening with ACT TWO, and so on.

Writer Beware!

Episodic dramas usually run to sixty minutes and have four acts plus a teaser and tag. If the program is up for syndication possibilities, there may be five acts to accommodate more advertising breaks. The average script length is around forty-eight to fifty-four pages.

Download free TV scripts off the internet. Try and get your hands on a script from the show you are writing. That way you won't have to guess what the producers prefer. Always write scripts on currently running shows. Study what is on the air now, not yesterday. TV has changed significantly.

Tag and Teaser

This is a simple television vernacular to be learned. The first term is the teaser. This is a short opening segment (about a minute or so) that introduces the characters and implies the action that's coming up. Remember, this is television and a viewer can very easily switch channels.

- Make the teaser count, so that the viewer is interested enough to stick around, or at least keep flipping back.
- Once you've reached the end of your episode script, you have to create the opposite of a teaser, called a tag. A tag usually runs for a few minutes; its function is to wrap up the show and its resolution. Sometimes the tag is set up on a humorous, upbeat note.
- Sometimes there might be a voice-over doing a promo as in, "And now scenes from next week's episode."

It should be obvious how important it is to research the show or program you might be writing for, or even one you'd like to pitch for, before you put your fingers to the keyboard. If you are not experienced in judging the passage of time relative to the scene or segment you are writing, get yourself a stopwatch and start timing and making notes on the teasers and tags on other programs.

Wow! What a "Mow": Movie of the Week

A television network has the option of purchasing a blockbuster film from a studio, usually for an extortionate amount of money. Because the networks are under restrictions that dictate what is permissible to say and show on the air, these films then have to be edited for television. However, the networks have another option—they can commission their own made-for-television films. These movies are often known as Movies of the Week (MOWs).

In the short run, it costs the networks less to produce their own films to suit the conditions under which they can show them than it does buying from the studios. In addition to that, a brought-in block-buster has to be edited into the six- to eight-act structure to accommodate the networks' advertisements, thus adding to its initial cost. When the drawbacks are added up, the bottom line comes out, for once, on the side of the writer: more MOWs, more work.

Pitch Before You Ditch

Before you can try to be hired as a freelance scriptwriter or try to land a job as a writer on a series, you have to produce something that can be evaluated. Nobody is going to hire you just because you have all the enthusiasm in the world and figure how nice it would be to write for television. Not, that is, unless you happen to be the personal friend of a major stockholder in the company.

Keep in mind that nowadays the networks are permitted to produce their own TV series. They used to be prohibited from doing this. The fact that broadcast networks are now producers, of course, changes the playing field for writers. Cable and satellite networks are producing their own series as well, all of which should mean more potential work for writers.

Breaking In

It is almost obligatory to have an agent to break in to the episodic or situation comedy market. But whichever you want to make a pitch for, it is essential that you produce sample scripts. These are not to be treated as spec scripts you want to sell, but as samples of your work that demonstrate your talent and ability to produce. Now, it's important that you use some common sense here.

How would you look at a sample script if you were an executive on a successful show? Naturally, you would have a critical stance and would compare the submitted script to your show. So it's not a good idea to write a sample script for the existing show that you'd like to write for. There are enough roadblocks without creating any of your own. The answer is to have a script that's similar in theme to the ones on the show you'd like to work on, but not versions of the same.

Hit Trick

It can't be emphasized enough how important it is to keep studying the television programs you would like to work on. Start taping them, particularly the comedy ones. You then have the opportunity of fast-forwarding to check on the timing of the gags or situations.

The Formula

Before you start writing the script you are going to use as a sample of your work, try to get hold of the show's bible. It will tell you the limitations of the characters, what they can do and cannot do. It will describe the structure of the program and even give advice about the number of pages that should go to make each act. Some might even tell you that every fifteen pages in a seven-act structure, something exciting should happen, or some big conflict should occur—like a cliffhanger, to be resolved after the commercial break (to persuade the viewer not to switch channels, at least until they have the answers).

You will find out that this is not applicable if the program you are writing samples for is a cable show, as there is no need to make accommodation for advertising. Neither will you find restrictions of certain kinds of dialogue and action that are frowned upon. Some successful television scriptwriters, many of whom used to write exclusively for the movies, prefer to leave the networks alone because they feel the restrictions get in the way of their artistic ideals.

You will note that just as the plot point system in a three-act movie structure is the form, so the same philosophy exists in the seven-act structure of this type of programming for television. The similarities don't stop there. Once you have completed your sample scripts you are ready to pitch them, which is virtually identical to the way you would operate if you were pitching a spec film script to a movie producer in Hollywood.

The Production Cycle

As the networks tend to work to a production schedule, it makes sense to work around the way most of them produce. The development cycle is generally from fall to midwinter. This is when pilot scripts for new series are commissioned and developed. If you don't have an agent, then scour the trade papers, which run news on what's on the upcoming slate.

From January to April a few selected scripts are chosen for production as pilot episodes. This is a terrible time for the new script-writer if he/she has a script in contention, because she has to hang around wondering if the pilot is going to make the list for a production order. That doesn't mean you are suddenly in the business. Very few pilots make it to series status.

Most of what goes on in this period, and all through May, is beyond the scriptwriter's control. There will be people to whom the producers owe a big favor, there will be stars who want or need work—in fact, any one of a whole list of people who have degrees of leverage will have far more influence than you on what pilot goes forward or not.

By September, some of the pilots make the broadcast schedule, but even these shows aren't considered home and dry. More and more, pilots are given only short production orders and if they don't make it with the audiences, say within four episodes, they are pulled in a hurry. Such is the competition, which has become fierce. By wintertime, wobbly series are being replaced by shows held in reserve for just such an occasion.

The Practical Stuff

Let's say that, wonder of wonders, the program executive liked your samples and is going to give you the opportunity of writing perhaps two scripts for the show. Now is the time for even more research; try to get hold of back episodes of the program. If it's a new show, that shouldn't be too difficult. Someone at the network or cable station can fix that for you. This is almost going to be like filling in a census form, and the answers are going to be just as important. What's the audience demographic (this should include the social strata)? What's the feel and style of the show? Is it lighthearted, serious, or does it deal with social issues?

How is the hour-long program filled out? Is there one solid plot line or subplots? Study the major characters until you know them like your relatives. Are there back stories to the characters? If so, do they have relevance to their lives now? Make a list of all the plot lines from previous episodes, just to be sure you don't repeat them.

Write What You Know

While you should have in mind the type of program you are going to write, so that the number of acts can be predicted, put that aside for a minute. When you are starting out it will probably be advantageous for you to write your spec work in the subject matter that is close to you and in which you feel most comfortable. Maybe you are really well-informed about crime stories, or medicine, or human nature stories—people in trouble and how they get out of it. Whichever, just keep it close to home.

Your feeling about the story will be reflected in your confidence, which, in turn, will be shown in your writing. A reader can tell if the writer is uncertain; it'll show. You are less likely to exhibit this lack of confidence if you stick to what you know. Later, when you are an ace, you can move on to any subject you like.

Writing for Young Audiences

The networks all aggressively seek out the same demographic audience, the eighteen- to thirty-four-year-old age group. In doing that, they have been copying the cable networks. This means producing what are called narrow-casting programs, which target that audience age group. These are the people advertisers love, and the programs that produce them are the ones in demand.

Scriptwriters are urged by their agents to come up with concepts that suit those criteria. At the same time, observers criticize the system that has media buyers who are under thirty-four constantly seeking the programs that fit only that demographic. A typical successful hit program that does fit the mold would be *Ally McBeal*, whose protagonist is in her twenties.

It stands to reason that as a general rule, like seeks like, so it should come as no surprise that the people who green-light pitches are, just as in the movies, in the same demographic as the intended audience. A gray-haired writer without a superb track record of success sitting across from someone who could be a son or daughter might not do too well.

Chapter 14

Catching and Trapping 'Em: Agents

Plan Your Attack

It is said that before you sell your first screenplay you should have written at least three. It is not required that you write them while hanging around the pool in Marina del Rey. You could very easily have been in a coffee bar in Billings, Montana. However, part of the education of a scriptwriter is how the business works and part of that is understanding, and perhaps being privy to, the undercurrent of snobbery and gossip that swirls around the best restaurant tables in Beverly Hills.

It would be wonderful if you could just call a studio, ask for an appointment, and take your brand-new spec screenplay in for a quiet discussion over a cup of tea. You may have been able to do it decades ago, but those days are long gone. Today, you can't just show up and expect to be heard. What you need is a marketing plan to get attention for yourself and your product. There's a long process to this stage as well, as you may well imagine. Read on to develop a strategy.

Word-of-Mouth: Techniques to Market

The most powerful advertising/sales tool is word of mouth. People trust their friends and what they tell them. Think about this example. Let's say a movie did really well and the studio decided to produce the sequel. Unfortunately, as it often happens, they couldn't get the same screenwriter and director, or maybe the sequel idea wasn't that great, but for one reason or another the end result was that the sequel turned out to be a bad film.

The first week the sequel was released at the movie theaters, many of the viewers who had seen the first film went to see the sequel, and so it did relatively well. But the following week, the attendance was way down. What happened? Word of mouth was to blame. The viewers who went the first week killed it.

Word of mouth works the other way, too. Once in a while there is an independently produced film that has no publicity budget and opens at a few art houses, and then catches on, until it gets distribution into the mainstream movie theaters. These late success stories are known as sleepers; sometimes it takes a while for word of mouth to spread from the water cooler to the rest of town.

You can use the concept of "word of mouth" in your marketing plan. Try to get your name out, so that people in the industry are talking about you and your work. With enough perseverance, you may generate enough interest for an interview with a studio executive and—who knows?—maybe even a contract deal.

Location, Location, Location

Using the word-of-mouth technique is difficult if you're not out in southern California. But don't give up your day job and move to Hollywood unless you suddenly come into a sizable amount of money.

If you live away from the typical American filmmaking areas, Los Angeles and New York, seriously consider using the agent route. Nevertheless, you still have to look at your personality. At the same time, take note of what your grandmother probably told you: "You can't make a silk purse out of a sow's ear." Be as honest as you can with yourself and don't try to be something you're not; be genuine.

The Out-of-Towners

It is a very nice idea to believe that talent will show and that all you need for success is for a reader in a prestigious agency or major studio to pick up your script and be absolutely overwhelmed by it. The problem is that if he or she sees an out-of-town postmark, the odds are that your friendly reader will suddenly be very much underwhelmed. Actually, it's terrible, but in a way understandable. Hollywood is a community that thinks only movies or television. Writing for movies requires a good understanding of how the business works, and to get that it helps if you live in the environs.

You will not add to your industry education by studying *People Magazine*, although if you think it's important you might get up to par on who is seeing whom. What would help would be to take subscriptions to "the trades." These are industry trade publications: *The Hollywood Reporter* and *Daily Variety*. There are now two versions available: print and Internet. You can start off by just looking around their Internet sites to get a feel, but to access any valuable information you have to subscribe.

The Power of Socializing

If you do happen to live relatively close to Hollywood or New York City, once you have completed your spec script the time has come to mix. You have to start talking, and anyone will do, from the nice man collecting the garbage (he may know people you would like to know), to your hairdresser, mail person, and even your dentist. Remember, many of those people have children who may go to school with the children of persons whom you would like to read your screenplay.

It is said that everyone in Hollywood has a screenplay in the works. But you'll also hear that people in the industry have only one topic of conversation. Along those lines, it would be a good idea to try and mix with below-the-line people. The two professions that have most insight into how pictures are made are cinematographers and editors. They know what will play and what will be cut.

Writer Beware!

Agents and managers are emphatic that ageism is not part of their way of doing business. But what about the people actually buying the material? One writer was known to make a point of sending his young son to meetings. The older man would write the stuff, while the younger one took care of the face-to-face pitching.

You could learn as much about writing a screenplay from the technical types on a film as you could from almost anyone else. Technicians tend to socialize with their own kind, and they have the inside track on all the gossip, a good cocktail party plus. In many ways, mixing with below-the-line people could be a far more rewarding experience, both practical and on a friendship basis, than with above-the-line people. The only competition a scriptwriter has is another scriptwriter.

Making Contacts

Contacts are the name of virtually every game. As the saying goes, "It's not what you know, it's who you know." That couldn't be more accurate than in the movie industry. The problem is most people don't have the right kind of movie contacts. That means you have to establish some.

The first step will be research; how can you get contacts if you don't know who to seek out? Doing the research necessary to produce contacts is rather like being a detective. The best detectives get their results from good and persistent legwork. In doing this kind of research it is very important to keep copious and accurate records.

Here is a list of major sources to try for contacts:

- Agents
- Managers
- Producers
- Production companies with deals at the major studios
- Independent producers
- Independent production companies that finance their own work
- Directors

And that's just a start—there's no reason to stop here. To make contacts you have to keep at it and not give up.

Socializing via the Internet

Maybe you could somehow strike up a friendship with some honest person in the general Los Angeles area (a possible alternative might be New York, which is fast becoming the hub for television, with movies on the side). The idea, of course, is that you can use this person's address as a mail drop. As this could turn out to be a burden on the lovely person, you could try an alternative.

The Internet, as most people know, means having an Internet Service Provider and a screen name. Your Internet address is, up to a point, anonymous, and if you want to get really cagey you could check the L.A. weather so you could drop remarks in your e-mail about the temperature and such. Just be sure you don't slip up and complain about the snow in Montana. There are other drawbacks that you face if you pull this kind of trick: attachments. Not too many agents or studios are going to accept them, which poses a problem with sending screenplays.

Again, the sensible way out of all this is to have an agent in the L.A. area who is not going to be thrown that you live several states away. He or she will be sensible enough not to bandy that you are not a local, and by the time your first script is being bid on, it won't matter. Once that happens, it will suddenly become the chic thing to have a screenwriter from Montana on the credits. In the end, for all the ploys everyone may use it is going to be the weight of your story that will tip the scales in your favor.

Cold Calling

Once you've done your research and your socializing, you'll have a few contact numbers. The next step is to call those people. Go over your script in your mind, so that you don't fluff on the phone, but be sure you aren't going to sound like a sales recording. Make notes on a pad to look at when you call someone, so you don't leave out any salient points you should be making. (Like what? Your log line, of course.) Set up some kind of record-keeping files on your computer, if you have one, to keep track of whom you call and what was discussed.

It's important not to rely solely on your memory, so make notes about personal matters as well as business ones. For instance, if a reader at a studio told you not to bother calling back because she would be off on vacation, ask her where she is going and when she'll be back. Make a note of the relevant dates so that you can call back at an appropriate time to find out how the holiday went.

You should be sure your telephone voice is friendly. Try to build up a relationship with the people you call. Of course, try not to overdo it—be casual, cool, and calm. The more calls you make, the better you'll get at them, so it's best to start out with the less important contact numbers.

Make Every Call Count

Whoever you speak to and whatever the results, always, always ask for a referral. Some people you speak to will give you a referral just to get you off the phone. That doesn't mean it's useless. When you do speak to the person to whom you were referred, give the source; for example: "So and so at Disney (or wherever) gave me your name and said you might be interested. . . ." If you draw a blank with this call, don't hang up until you have asked them, too, for a referral.

Always remember that the one person in an office who has the best information is the secretary. A good secretary knows everything that goes on and just may be your best contact. Being an intelligent person, you will always treat people on the other end of a telephone with respect. Never brush off a secretary or receptionist, or act like you're some superstar; as far as you are concerned, the secretary is frequently the most important person in the company.

Snail Mail

Another way to contact the studios is to send them your work by mail. One rejection-reducing device is to be sure you send your work to someone who might be in the market for it and thus be sympathetic. For example, it would probably not be a good ploy to send your spec script on the voluntary destruction of all armaments to the head of the NRA (National Rifle Association) film department. It's useless to send an adult film that may get an NC-17 rating to Disney, so make sure you do your research and find out which studios and producers may be interested in your particular line of work.

The Query Letter

There are many people who think query letters are a waste of time. Their reasoning is that if a query letter arrives on a producer's desk, the secretary is going to open it, take one look, and either throw it in the wastebasket or, if there is a SASE envelope enclosed, send back a template rejection letter. In many cases, that is exactly what happens—but sometimes a query letter can make a huge difference in the life of a screenwriter, so it may be advisable to take your chances.

It might be worthwhile to consider the psychology of the situation. Without scripts, movies would not be made and studios would not stay in business. People in the moviemaking business need ideas and scripts—as long as these are ideas and scripts that will make movies that sell. What they really want, of course, is to latch on to a better script than the competition.

All moviemakers are bombarded with outlines, synopses, endless log lines, and scripts, most of which come via agents. Word travels very quickly in the industry and pretty soon almost everyone knows what is doing the rounds. What they would all die for is the idealistic dream: An envelope is opened and out of it come a few typed pages. The recipient picks them up and starts to read what they figure is yet another piece of nonsense. Just a minute, they think, this is good—this is very good. Who is this person?

The interesting thing about this little piece of daydreaming is that both sides have it: the writer and the producer. The more sophisticated they are the less they believe it will ever happen, but the idea of it never really fades. The reason is that it has actually happened, therefore the thinking is, it could happen again—and so it could, and why not with your script?

And Here's the Pitch

You are now fully prepared to make your pitch. You have all the material written and completed, you have rehearsed it with your friends and enemies, and you have been working endlessly generating contacts. Now one of them agrees to see you. It's what you have worked toward: the pitch.

You have read up about how to handle a pitch and talked to your contacts and quizzed people about what to expect. Being the movie business, of course, a relatively simple business meeting has been blown up into something rather more dramatic. Although it is true that the outcome could mean an awful lot of money for the scriptwriter.

Some advisors have said that the writer should be emotional about the story, even to the point of making a fool of himself or herself. Some have even suggested that if a writer has difficulty in handling an audience, they should take acting classes.

Hit Trick

"Not memorizing your pitch is important, because if you fumble or get confused and have to make unexpected decisions during the pitch, you'll look very uncertain. The way you present yourself has a lot to do with how much the buyer has confidence that you'll be able to write what you're pitching." —Ron Bass, an American screenwriter. His films include, but are not limited to, **Passion of Mind**, **Snow Falling on Cedars**, **Entrapment**, and **Stepmom**.

What it comes down to, yet again, is personality and what kind you may have. Of course, it also comes down to how hungry you are and how far you are prepared to go.

Relying on the Log Line

There is no doubt about it, there are a lot of young people about and many of them seem to have a job that revolves around running a studio in Hollywood, or that's the way it appears. Along with youth comes the short attention span. There is no point sitting around bemoaning that fact, you just have to operate in a way that turns it to your advantage. A major factor in that endeavor is brevity, or keep it short with punch, or as Mr. Eastwood has said: "Cut to the chase."

To the folks that you are pitching to their time is at a premium. Hence the idea of "concept" becomes essential, and you have to spend time learning and honing one of those to sell your script. There are concept guidelines: Tell your story and its hook in twenty-five words or less. This takes us back to the Hollywood staple: log line and outline.

A log line is the selling pitch that encapsulates the absolute essence of your story. (Tip: Don't use long words like "encapsulates" in your log line. It has too many syllables in it.) Another way of looking in at the contents of a log line would be to visualize it as if it were in the poster for the picture. Naturally, these have a technical name, which came from the people who make the posters: One-Sheet.

You will see posters in frames on the walls of your local cinema, under "Coming Soon" or something like that. It's typical that the poster will have a picture of the lead actor(s) against a background that should give the viewer a good idea of the type of film being advertised. Then there might also be a line or two of type in the poster layout. It's that text that could have been your log line, although in reality, of course, had it been, the log line would have come a long time before the poster for the produced picture.

Sometimes there will be log line–type text in newspaper advertisements. Generally, though, the text will be crowded out by quotes from reviews that are being used to promote the picture. Here are a few log line examples taken from actual film posters:

- **Independence Day:** "Aliens try to invade earth on Independence Day."
- **Liar, Liar:** "An attorney, because of a birthday wish, can't tell any lies for 24 hours."
- **The Recruit with Al Pacino:** "Trust, Betrayal, Deception. In the C.I.A. Nothing Is What It Seems."
- **Murder by Numbers with Sandra Bullock:** "Let the Mind Games Begin."
- **Insomnia with Al Pacino and Robin Williams:** "Tough Cop. Brilliant Killer. Unspeakable Crime."
- **Dreamcatcher with Morgan Freeman:** "Four Friends Hang a Dreamcatcher in Their Cabin. It's About to Catch Something It Cannot Stop."
- **25th Hour with Edward Norton:** "Can You Change Your Whole Life in a Day?"

Keep in mind that those lines of text were written by professionals. When you come to write your log line, try to emulate the style of the professionals. Just as the poster was written and designed to entice people to want to see the picture, so your log line should be designed so that your audience, the Hollywood reader, is persuaded to read your spec script.

The Agents

Agents are like salespeople who work on commission. If they get you a deal and sell your screenplay, they'll get a part of whatever you get from the studios—generally around 10 percent. That is why they are so picky about who they represent. If they see no chance of your work ever making it, they won't waste their time representing you.

However, if they do recognize your potential, they will do all the marketing, contracting, and negotiations for you, while you're free to begin writing another script. And if you are lucky, a good agent may also offer you advice; if any of them do, seriously consider taking it.

Writer Beware!

Most agent/writer contracts have a clause where each can give a three-month termination notice. Agents typically want new clients to sign for a specified period—six months to a year is not unusual. If an agent isn't getting anywhere after three months, they tend to cool off. Tip: Never bug your agent.

Agents aren't writers, but if they are any good they know what sells and how to sell it. Agents can be the making of your career and they can be the biggest pain, maybe both at the same time. Nevertheless, whatever you think of agents you are going to need one, unless you were brought up in the film industry and have a degree in law.

If you do not live in the Los Angeles or New York City areas, an agent is going to be essential. Actually, even if you do live there you are probably going to need one just the same. You should understand a few things about the breed. They are commission-only salespeople. If any so-called agent asks for payments or fees in advance, be very wary and keep looking.

The Managers

You can have both an agent and a manager or one or the other. Obviously, to have both is a fair indication that you might be doing quite well. Or it could mean that you will lose more money in commission, because a manager is paid on the same basis as the agent— the manager's cut is usually 15 percent, though rates do vary.

The theory about managers is that the service the client gets tends to be more personal, or at least that's what managers say. Many sit down with the client and draft out a plan of action that may cover one, two, or more years. Managers, more than most agents, will offer writing advice to their writers, which you might think is a good introduction to a business where other people tinkering with your material is the standard.

The Manager's Role

There's nothing wrong with managers hawking and selling a screenplay. However, they are supposed to have a lawyer on the phone when the negotiating is in progress. Obviously, the manager/ writer relationship is a delicate one. But it can be a very valuable one because managers frequently handle the careers of directors. It doesn't take a brain surgeon to work out that having writers and directors in the same camp can prove to be synergistic.

How to Find a Good Agent

Once you are hired or contracted to either sell your spec script or write one, it shouldn't be difficult to find an agent; after all, you will be handing them 10 percent of something. But what if you don't have a deal yet? It's still possible to find an agent even before you do any selling on your own.

The best way to find a good doctor, lawyer, dentist, or plumber is to have one recommended to you by a friend whose opinion you trust. It's the same with agents. However, the odds are that you don't have a friend who has an agent. And even if you did have one, some friends aren't too keen on recommending other friends to their agent; they tend to be possessive about them.

Those dear friends of yours will tell you such things as, "My agent has closed his/her books and isn't taking on any new clients." Do not despair—all is not lost. There are a number of reference books and Web sites you can research. (See Appendix B for details.) But before we move on to how you can find the right agent, there are a couple of things you should know.

Reputable or Not?

No reputable agent would ever require payment other than for preapproved expenses. No self-respecting agent would ever charge reading or service fees, and most of the agents out there do abide by this unspoken rule. If your agent ever refers to another person or business that specializes in script doctoring, be aware that something shady may be going on. The most likely explanation is that the script doctor is your agent's cousin and needs an extra project to pay the bills.

It's Time to Begin Your Search

Getting an agent is not easy. It would be lovely if all you had to do was to pick one from the reference books and put in a call. Unfortunately, it's going to take more effort than that. First of all, you should tackle the problem that even well-established writers have had to face: whether you want to work with a big-shot agent or one who's just starting out.

Would you prefer to be handled by one of the prestige giants like William Morris, who, it is argued, can use his clout because of the megastars he handles to push your product? A big-name agent like that has easy access at many studios and can certainly get your script seen, but will he have the time to do that? Or is he more likely to file it away and concentrate on his big-name clients, who are a sure bet when it comes to getting his commission?

On the other hand, a relatively unknown agent may have more of an interest in selling your screenplay and give you more attention. After all, he, too, is trying to make a name for himself in the business. But there are downsides as well. For one thing, an inexperienced agent may hurt rather than help a screenwriting career with just a few false moves. And in his eagerness for projects, a small-time agent may take on too many clients and end up with little time for each one.

You don't always get to pick your agent—it's hard enough just to find one—but keep in mind that settling for an agent that you're not happy with isn't the best course of action. Make sure that the agent you find is right for you, that you can work well together, and that you have at least some trust in what he's doing on your behalf.

Hitting the Books

Let's say you have all the reference books in front of you and you start going through them in an effort to find an agent you think might be good for you. It's a bit like picking racehorses. Some people like finding fun coincidences, while others begin with the letter A and go down from there.

What you should understand is that the entries in the reference books are based on information given to the publisher by the agent—that is, this isn't someone else's reference of the agent, it's what the agent chose to say about herself. This means that you won't see anything negative—but you'll also get lots of valuable information that you should pay attention to. For instance, if the entry tells you the agent doesn't handle animation, don't waste her time and yours by sending her an outline of your updated version of *Snow White and the Seven Dwarfs*.

What you can do is check the entry against the agent's name where it says when the agency was established. If it's 1952, obviously the outfit has been around for a fair time; if it's 2002, that's a different matter. You might presume that the longer-established agency has wiser agents and a longer credit list of successes. On the other hand, the young one might be better for you; maybe the agents in the newer agency are hip and cool and eager to prove themselves in the industry.

Working the Phones

Agents are generally available on the phone, except for the superagents who tend to be snooty and unavailable. Nevertheless, it would be a good idea to start calling around when you begin looking for representation. Do not presume you are going to have a heart-to-heart chat with an agent about your career. Try that and you will find the call has come to a sudden end; agents are busy people.

What can get you into a conversation is to say to the agent or her assistant/secretary that you are a new scriptwriter seeking representation and inquire whether they are taking on new clients. The standard reply is that yes, they always consider new talent. This will be followed by a request that you send in a query letter and an outline.

But you might hit them on a slow day and they could ask you what your project is about. Bingo, now you have a chance to talk about your work. Don't start going off on an hour-long lecture—just give them your log line and the first paragraph you worked so hard on, and see where the conversation takes you. Chances are it will end up with the same query letter/outline request.

What you accomplish by telling the agent about your work is that you have increased the chances of having your material read instead of languishing in the pending/unsolicited file—after all, it's now been requested. So when you send in that letter, be sure you have the person's name—spelled correctly—and address your query letter to him or her personally; make reference to your telephone conversation. To be on the safe side, print "Requested Material" on the outside of the envelope.

The Query Letter

Even if you don't get that personal conversation, sending a query letter is still a well-established method. Keep your query letter to a page and forget any funny stuff designed to get the reader's attention, like colors, drawings, and smart-aleck remarks. If you were an agent, how many pages of a query letter would you have time to plow through? Not too many, if you could help it.

The query letter should contain a brief cover letter that will mention your pertinent career accomplishments and the purpose of your writing. To the cover letter, you will attach the outline or treatment and a self-addressed stamped envelope, so that the agent may send you a reply.

If you find that you aren't getting any positive responses to your query letters, there a few simple factors that might be holding you back: Do you make sure that the agent you are addressing is still with the agency where you are sending your query letter? Agents move around in the industry and that agent may have gone elsewhere. Do you write to "Dear Agent," instead of finding out the correct name? Do you take care to spell the agent's name correctly? Do you tell the potential agent what a wonderful writer you are?

Any one of these mistakes will get a writer a rejection slip. It may be that it is not the fault of the agent but of the writer that is causing all the rejections. There is a proper and an improper way of doing business that comes before an agent gets down to reading a spec screenplay. Make sure you aren't shortchanging yourself.

Once You Have an Agent

When you get an agent, keep in mind that first there's the honeymoon; so now when you go to cocktail parties you can make remarks like, "Yeah, well, according to my agent. . . . " Having an agent puts you up a few rungs in the industry.

However, it will be your work that will keep you there and with hope will cement your relationship with your agent, so that the honeymoon turns out to be a long-term arrangement.

And it's important not to forget that the agent/writer relationship should always remain a business relationship, and that each one of you should have your best interests in mind, especially when it comes to paying your agent commission.

Contract and Commission

The agent's income today is calculated at the rate of 10 percent of whatever they sell, which is less than literary agents, who earn 15 percent (the rate goes up to 20 percent if foreign manuscript sales are involved). If they don't do it themselves, many literary agents have correspondent agents who handle film sales. The rule of thumb is that generally the size of the agency will dictate their involvement, and the degree of it, in film sales. Film agents who belong to the Society of Authors' Representatives are prohibited from charging more than 10 percent commission.

Hit Trick

"Do really good work. Be self-critical and make changes they don't expect you to make. If you can take their notes in your own way, you'll both be happy . . . . If you don't like the notes, or you are defensive and arrogant about taking them, you're not going to last . . . . If you realize the project is becoming the movie you didn't want to make, and you don't think it'll work, it's perfectly okay to walk away. I've done it." —Leslie Dixon, screenwriter. Her films include, but are not limited to, **Hairspray**, **Just Like Heaven**, **Freaky Friday**, and **The Thomas Crown Affair**.

The contract between an author and an agent typically contains a clause that the agent collects money on behalf of the writer. The agent then takes his commission before passing on the rest of the money to the writer. You might ask: Why doesn't the author get paid in full, then pay his or her agent the commission? One reason might be that authors can be funny people who can come up with all sorts of reasons why the agent isn't worth the commission. The authors in those cases tend to conveniently forget that without the agent they wouldn't have a sale. All of which makes it very clear why the agent should collect the money and pay the author.

Another question might be: Supposing the agent does get paid, then takes off for some island in the Pacific with all my money? Seeing that such action is a big-time offense and would ruin an agent's career, to say nothing of possible incarceration, it's highly unlikely to happen. There is an alternative if you are worried, and that's to work with an entertainment attorney. Some lawyers work by the hour, in which case the writer would receive the money and the lawyer would bill the writer for the hours worked.

Beware of the Fee-Charging Agent

The first red flag that signifies someone is after your money and not your ability to write screenplays is when a reply comes back to a standard submission and query: "We thought what you sent us had strong possibilities. However, like a lot of screenplays circulating today, it does need some polishing. We would suggest. . . ." It's your wallet they want to polish, not your screenplay. The trouble is compounded if you bite and get involved with these people; the fees due will keep piling up along with the edits.

If You Can't Beat 'Em: Becoming an Agent

There's always a bright side. If you can't find an agent, why not become one yourself? You'll gains tons of experience in the industry, make a few sales, and then—who knows?—maybe the experience will teach you how you can improve your own work. Then, you can one day give up your agenting career and go back to screenwriting.

Imagine you are an agent. You might work in one of the classy and very large outfits in an upscale Beverly Hills office, or you might work out of your home. Essentially, wherever you work, you do the same thing: evaluate properties and try to sell them. That, of course, is an oversimplification, but no matter how you dress it up, it's very close to the bottom line of the job.

Basically anyone can become an agent; all they have to do if they live and operate in California is to become licensed and bonded with the State Labor Commission. (Other states have similar regulations.) While not a requirement, it is important to the client that the agent is a WGA (Writers Guild of America) signatory. Wherever you live, check the qualifications, memberships, and whatever state licensing requirements are in force.

The most important part of being an agent is knowing the industry—and making sure that the industry knows you. It's fairly typical that new agents are spinoffs from other larger agencies and often bring existing clients with them. In publishing it's common for editors to turn to being agents; the money is better. It stands to reason that for any agent to be a success, they have to be connected; this is particularly so in Hollywood.

An agent is only as good as his or her reputation, and he or she builds a reputation by discovering winners. That's why agents are so picky about taking on new clients and their work. The worst thing an agent can do is to send a studio a clunker of a script with a buildup that trumpets it's the next *Die Hard* when it's really a sad knockoff. The agent vouches for the integrity of each script he or she represents.

Chapter 15

What the Future Holds

What to Expect When You're Expecting a Film

There is a very nice middle-aged lady who lives in a good-sized cabin in the middle of the High Sierras in California with her dog. This lady happens to be an excellent screenwriter. She doesn't drink very much, she gave up smoking and loud men, and she gets on very well with her two grown-up children. When people meet her for the first time they find it hard to believe what she does for a living. If you were to create a scriptwriter as a character for your film, it's doubtful if he or she would fit this image. Well, not all Italians are in the Mafia either.

Hit Trick!

"Be patient, keep your fingers crossed, and believe your ideas are viable and valuable. Even though 'they' don't want what you just wrote this week, the tide will turn, believe me, and it can turn on a dime." —Steven DeSouza, and american screenwriter; his films include, **The Ghost Who Walks**, **Return of the Ninja**, **Isobar**, and **Street Fighter**.

A screenwriter can have a wonderful life; the work is very rewarding, the pay—when it comes—is pretty good, too; and you can meet some very interesting people in this line of work.

A "Real" Screenwriter

Many people wonder what a "real" screenwriter looks like and where these people live. The odd thing is, most screenwriters are probably very much like you. Sure, there are a few who live in Hollywood, drink too much, have wild parties, and are constantly surrounded by film industry people, but this isn't the case for everyone.

However, there are some distinctions that are common to those of the screenwriting profession. Imagination, inquisitiveness, and open-mindedness, though they are becoming rarer, are the traits of the best screenwriters. Screenwriters seek after realism, and many are inspired by an urge to comment on the human condition, coupled with a need to seek out the original and tell a good story.

You may think that it takes years to earn the title of screenwriter, but screenwriting careers are made in Hollywood every day. Screenplay acceptances and contracts do happen, to first-timers as well as experienced writers—but you've got to make them happen. It will take a huge amount of work as well as determination, patience, and, in some cases, luck, but the opportunities are there—you just have to seize them. Once you do, your biggest worry will be how to deal with all that good fortune and success.

The Ups and Downs and How to Deal

Screenwriters must be careful about success and failure; a strong reaction to either one can destroy a career and even a life. Celebrity is to be avoided at all costs; that comes easier to writers than many others, because the genuine ones don't need to be known.

Living with Success

Like many of the very good they are always uncertain of their talent; they have learned the value of humility.

More than anything they are grateful that they have found a way to write that rewards them not only in the way they might have thought when they started out, with money, but with the knowledge that the best in everything is simplicity. The best writer is a simple soul aiming to please, which might be why it is easy to take advantage of writers. It was written that the pen is mightier than the sword. Wield it well if you can.

Writer Beware!

Try to form a screenwriter's group. Aim to have four or five members—keep the membership low and try to find serious people. If it's possible, arrange to meet at each other's homes every two weeks or so. Make it plain that the group welcomes honest opinions, but that courtesy should be kept.

Dealing with Rejection

Of course, the flip side of success and celebrity is rejection. As the statistics combed from the literature of psychoanalysts tell us, rejection is a big number in the mental health problem department. Unfortunately, when you are a writer of any kind, rejection is part and parcel of the game. If in times of stress you are attracted to high places like the Golden Gate Bridge, perhaps you should consider another line of work.

Even if you think you can handle rejection, always remember that people judging your work are totally subjective and their rejection may have less to do with the actual script than with a number of other factors, some of which have nothing to do with you.

Learning from It!

When it comes to rejection, the only thing you can do is learn from it. If you get form rejections, it's still worth the effort to call the agents/producers and in a charming manner ask if on your next submission they could kindly offer some advice along with their rejection. You'll be surprised at their reaction.

A modern playwright of some renown has said that he never sends in a play to be read, he always "performs" it. In fact, not one of his plays that have been on Broadway got anywhere with a producer until he "performed" it. That's worth thinking about. At the risk of boring some of your friends, you might try out your screenplay by reading it to them. The other advantage to "performing" your screenplays, even to an audience of one (you), is that you will get to know how it "plays."

What the Critics Say

Even if your script is accepted by the studio for production, there is another form of rejection—one that is more public and arguably more difficult to deal with. It's the rejection of the film critic or film reviewer, who proclaims a film as a failure.

If anyone wants to judge the effectiveness of critics, think of the many times one has praised a film as Oscar potential and when you came out of the cinema after seeing it you wondered if the critic was talking about the same film. This isn't to say the critic was wrong, only that you and the critic didn't get the same message from the picture.

Hit Trick

"Don't mind criticism. If it's untrue, disregard it; if it's unfair, keep from irritation; if it's ignorant, smile; if it's justified, learn from it." —Anonymous.

Once you've had your screenplay accepted and it is in production, there will come the day when it is released (some might say "escaped"), and the reviews of it hit the newsstands. While you may be a stoic sort of person, completely well-balanced and not subject to self-doubt and self-recrimination, these reviews, nevertheless, can have a tremendous effect. Not so much on your current well-being, but on your Hollywood future.

You've Made It! What You Can Expect to Make in Return

It's not unreasonable to wonder how much you might be paid for writing something that could end up being used in a film or television production. The trouble is that, like a lot of things, only the most extravagant tales reach the columns of the newspapers.

Most people have read an item that says so and so was paid some extraordinary amount of money for scripting such and such a film and when is all this gross-flowing river of money ever going to stop? Well, for most scriptwriters it never started.

Minimum Wage

While there is no minimum wage laid out, the WGA does publish the WGA Theatrical and Television Basic Agreement, which includes a section on "Theatrical Compensation." Original screenplay and treatment travels from a recommended low of nearly $50,000 to a high of about $100,000.

In addition to the Basic Agreement there is also something called the WGA Low Budget Agreement Fact Sheet. It may not apply to you, but you never know; however, it does give you another yardstick against which to judge what you may be offered.

The first two points read:

1. The Low Budget Agreement is offered to WGA members and nonmembers for purchases of existing screenplays and one rewrite. It is not for development.
2. The agreement applies to films budgeted at $750,000 and below.

From that point onward it is suggested that you call your lawyer. It should be noted that a freelance scriptwriter is generally classified by the IRS as a self-employed person. Of course, this may not apply to you, but either way it might be prudent to consult your local IRS advisor, who can tell you about nasty things like self-employment tax and what sort of genuine expenses you can claim.

Deals and Doctors (Script Doctor, That Is)

New and well-established writers may receive money for their scripts in different ways as well. The next section details money exchanges whether you are starting off, and someone is taking a chance on you, or you are an expert, and someone is asking your advice.

Development Deals

Sometimes a writer is offered a development deal, or step deal. This means that the scriptwriter receives an advance, then more money as he or she moves through the script-development stages step by step.

Writer Beware!

Every spacecraft that zooms away from a planet about to implode, every monster that wields a bloody axe, every gun that spouts bullets, every fire that consumes buildings, every miracle that saves a life, every laugh that warms a soul, every hero who rides into the valley and every villain who leaves; all of these emanate from the pen of the screenwriter.

It is not uncommon for the process to grind to a halt. When that happens, you are said to be "mired in development hell."

There have been many writers who have made a very good living out of writing scripts that go through the development process only to end up as scrapped projects. In such cases, the advance is the writer's consolation prize for the time and effort spent on writing the screenplay that will never make it to the silver screen.

Script Doctors

In Hollywood there are veteran writers who are well-known for being experts in certain elements of a screenplay, such as dialogue, action, love scenes, and so on. These writers have built reputations writing in the same limited vein over and over. They aren't asked to write action if they have the reputation for writing dialogue, or the other way around. Basically, they are specialists, and they are sometimes called upon by the studios to fix a script that is lacking in one area.

These writers, known as script doctors, do exactly what their job title implies—they fix the parts of the script that aren't done right, doctoring the flow, dialogue, scene structure, and so forth. Script doctoring can be a highly paid occupation; many of them earn more than real doctors.

If you are better at editing than creating original work, you may consider script doctoring as an alternative career option. Of course, the screenplays you'd work on would never carry your name, but you'd get a lot more projects that actually make it to the screen, and you'll get valuable experience along the way.

Directing Your Own

If a writer is working with a studio and/or a producer or director, then he or she will have to learn the art of compromise. There is only one situation where the scriptwriter can have anything approaching control and that's if he or she directs the film as well as writes it.

Many writers work toward directing, even though in the early days directors were looked on as technicians, certainly not artists. It was the French who changed that opinion when they proposed their principle of the auteur. (Woody Allen is a good example of an American auteur.) In spite of that, there are many highly experienced and talented writers who hold to the opinion that almost anyone in the business can do what a director does. However, very few directors can do what the people they control do: cinematographers, editors, sound editors, to name only three of the most important.

Appendix A

Glossary

When it comes to screenwriting, it helps to know the lingo. You can use the following glossary to see how much you already know and brush up on the terms that you may have forgotten.

action: The text in the script that appears flush left and provides background information as well as the action taking place on the screen. This text should be concise and refer to what the audience would see and hear.

back story: Information about a character's past that helps viewers to better understand the story.

conflict: In terms of the screenplay, conflict provides tension and builds the dramatic action, leading up to confrontation and eventually resolution.

copyright: Legal ownership of written material, including the right of reproduction.

crisis: A point when two or more forces confront each other.

denouement: The period that follows the climax, when any remaining issues are resolved.

dramatic action: The progression of the plot that drives the story line through the plot points and on to a resolution.

exposition: The parts of a script that show what happened previously and identify the characters and the time and place of the action. Exposition shouldn't be spelled out by the characters but be an invisible part of the story.

genre: Film category such as drama, comedy, and action. Many genres may be subdivided into subgenres—comedy may be a romantic comedy, slapstick, or a parody.

Hollywood: A town in southern California, Hollywood has become a catch-all term for the American film industry.

indie: Independent filmmaker, studio, or producer; indies generally have smaller budgets and frequently make films that are considered "artsy" as opposed to commercial or mainstream.

log line: A compelling one-liner or two-line description of a screenplay that will help you sell your idea.

master scene: All the action and dialogue that occurs within one setting at a particular time.

"meets" line: A one-liner that describes a film by using the "meets" formula—for instance, you may describe a new frat house comedy with the following "meets" line: *"Animal House* meets *There's Something About Mary."*

parenthetical: In a script, a word or phrase in parentheses between the character's name and the dialogue line, which provides information about how the dialogue is spoken.

plot: What happens in the movie.

plot point: A particular occurrence within a script when something happens to change the direction of the story.

prop: An object used by the actors in a scene; one of the most common props in today's movies is the phone.

scenario: See shooting script.

scene: One event in a screenplay, with a beginning, a middle, and an end; a scene often contains a crisis or confrontation and always advances the story.

scene transition: In the script, you move from scene to scene by way of a scene transition, set in all caps and appearing in the right margin; your basic options with scene transition are DISSOLVE TO, CUT TO, and FADE TO BLACK.

shooting script: A detailed script written for film production (particularly the director and camera crew). It includes camera shots and other material not appropriate for the spec script.

slug-line: Identifies the time and location of a scene. INT. (interior) and EXT. (exterior) indicate whether the scene is taking place inside or outside. NIGHT or DAY indicate the time of day. For example: INT. LIVING ROOM – NIGHT. The slug line information is always given in capital letters.

spec script: The basic form of a script used to sell the film idea; unlike a shooting script, it does not contain shooting details like camera angles.

storyboard: Sketches of a script's scenes that the director uses to plan the making of the film.

subtext: The thoughts and motivations that influence the characters, even though they are never directly expressed.

synopsis: Detailed outline of the film, scene by scene, but without the dialogue.

three-act structures: Most film scripts (as well as theater plays) may be divided into three acts; the first act introduces the story and character, the second act moves the story forward through the plot points and develops the characters, and the third act provides the resolution.

treatment: A breakdown of a story that describes it in just a few pages. Often a producer who is considering a script will ask to have a treatment written to sell him or her on the story.

voice-over (V.O.): Commentary by a character or narrator that is heard from off-screen or that is set up as a character's thoughts.

Additional Resources/Further Reading

Books

Biskind, Peter. *Easy Riders, Raging Bulls: How the Sex-Drugs-and-Rock 'n' Roll Generation Saved Hollywood.* New York: Simon & Schuster, 1999.

Crowe, Cameron. *Conversations with Wilder.* New York: Alfred A. Knopf, 1999.

Field, Syd. *Screenplay: The Foundations of Screenwriting.* Third edition. Fine Publications, 1994.

———. *Four Screenplays: Studies in the American Screenplay.* New York: Dell Trade Paperback, 1994.

Hampe, Barry. *Making Documentary Films and Reality Videos.* New York: Owl Books, 1997.

Harmetz, Aljean. *The Making of Casablanca: Bogart, Bergman, and World War II.* New York: Hyperion Books, 2002.

Iglesias, Karl. *The 101 Habits of Highly Successful Screenwriters: Insider's Secrets from Hollywood's Top Writers.* Avon, MA: Adams Media Corporation, 2001.

Keane, Christopher. *How to Write a Selling Screenplay: A Step-by-Step Approach to Developing Your Story and Writing Your*

Screenplay by One of Today's Most Successful Screenwriters and Teachers. New York: Bantam Doubleday Dell Publication, 1998.

Litwak, Mark. *Reel Power: The Struggle for Influence and Success in the New Hollywood.* Los Angeles: Silman-James Press, 1994.

O'Donnell, Pierce and Dennis McDougal. *Fatal Subtraction. How Hollywood Really Does Business.* New York: Doubleday, 1992.

Parkinson, David. *History of Film.* New York: Thames and Hudson, Inc., 1996.

Salamon, Julie. *The Devil's Candy. The Anatomy of a Hollywood Fiasco.* Cambridge, MA: DaCapo Press, 2002.

Straczynski, Michael J. *The Complete Book of Scriptwriting.* Cincinnati, OH: Writer's Digest Books, 2002.

Trottier, David. *The Screenwriter's Bible: A Complete Guide to Writing, Formatting, and Selling Your Script.* Third Edition. Los Angeles, CA: Silman-James Press, 1998.

Wilder, Billy. *Double Indemnity: The Complete Screenplay.* Berkeley, CA: University of California Press, 2000.

———. *Sunset Boulevard: The Complete Screenplay.* Berkeley, CA: University of California Press, 1999.

Wilen, Lydia and Joan Wilen. *How to Sell Your Screenplay: A Realistic Guide to Getting a Television or Film Deal.* New York: Square One Publishers, 2001.

Winokur, Jon. *Writers on Writing.* Third edition. Philadelphia, PA: Running Press Book Publishers, 1990.

Periodicals

Daily Variety
5700 Wilshire Blvd, Suite 120
Los Angeles, CA 90036
(323) 857-6600
www.variety.com

Hollywood Scriptwriter
P.O. Box 10277
Burbank, CA 91510
www.hollywoodscriptwriter.com

The Hollywood Reporter
5055 Wilshire Blvd.
Los Angeles, CA 90036
(323) 525-2000
www.hollywoodreporter.com

Professional Organizations

Writers Guild of America, East
555 West 55th Street, Suite 1230
New York, NY 10019-2967
(212) 767-7800
www.wgaeast.org

U.S. Copyright Office
Library of Congress
101 Independence Avenue, SE
Washington, DC 20559-6000
(202) 707-3000 (Information)

Writers Guild of America, West
7000 West 3rd Street
Los Angeles, CA 90048-4329
(323) 951-4000
www.wga.org

Academy of Motion Picture
Arts and Sciences
8949 Wilshire Blvd
Beverly Hills, CA 90211-1972
(310) 247-3000
www.oscars.org

Sample Material and Formatting Guidelines

This appendix contains sample materials for the film *The Swing Sisters*, including the screenplay cover page and a sample scene sequence, which you may use for your reference. You will also find a general formatting outline to help with all of your formatting needs.

(Name of Project)

by
(Name of First Writer)

(Based on, If Any)

Revisions by
(Names of Subsequent Writers,
in order of Work Performed)

Current Revisions by
(Current Writer, date)

Name (of company, if applicable)
Address
Phone Number
Sample Scene Sequence:

[EXT]FADE IN:
EXT. PRESERVATION HALL - NIGHT

Jazz coming from inside.

Superimposed on screen: New Orleans, 1918

INT. preservation hall - NIGHT

"Papa" Jack's Reliance Band is blowing the roof off. The
audience, like the band, is mostly black. JACK JEROME, a
white trumpet player jams on his horn. In jazz it's not the
color of your skin, it's how you play. Jack is one of the
best.

JEANNIE (V.O.)
My Daddy blew the horn. He played with
the best of them: Jelly Roll Mortin,
Papa Jack, Pops Foster, even Armstrong
himself. . . .

At the back of the room are two sleeping white kids, BILLY,
4, and JEANNIE, 6. The loud music has no effect on them.

JEANNIE (V.O.) (cont'd)
We never talked about our mother or
why she left, but it was always just
the three of us. We lived near the
French Quarter. Then when New Orleans
jazz became the national rage, our
home was the road. Billy was four and
I was six.

EXT. french quarter - day

An old Model T is packed to the hilt. Jeannie puts Billy in
the front seat, then gets in the back. Jack takes a quick
hit from a flask, gets behind the wheel, lights up, and
they're off.

JEANNIE (V.O)
Our summers were filled with endless
days of driving and long nights in
clubs.

Various shots

The Model T passes billboards for Coca-Cola . . . I'd Walk
A Mile For a Camel. Jazz plays over - "Sweet Georgia Brown,"
or some such.

JEANNIE (V.O.)
When school was in Dad got gigs that
lasted longer, but just when it began
to feel like home, it was time for
another town. . . .

EXT. A DESERTED COUNTRY ROAD - DAY

The trio in the Model T. It's blazing hot. Jack lights up another smoke and wipes his sweat. Jeannie and Billy, a couple years older, look bored and exhausted.

>   BILLY
>   It's gonna get better.

>   JEANNIE
>   Says who?

>   BILLY
>   Krazy Cat.

>   JEANNIE
>   Did not.

>   BILLY
>   Did, too. He said it when he waged war
>   against the mice.

EXT. CHICAGO STREETs - WINTER - DAY

The kids bundled up together in the back. Jack takes a hit of fortification to stay warm.

>   JEANNIE (V.O.)
>   There was talk of "The Red Summer,"
>   and race riots. . . .

Insert - quick freeze frames

Interracial violence in Tulsa and St. Louis . . . white mobs setting fire to black districts . . . clashes in the streets.

>   JEANNIE
>   . . . but that's not the world we
>   saw.

Int. SOUTH SIDE speakeasy - NIGHT

A "black-and-tans," Southside club catering to both black
and "slummers," middle- and upper-class whites, is the hot-
test ticket in town. Jack on stage with a black quintet jams
on the "Twelfth Street Rag." Bouncers man the doors.

                    JEANNIE (V.O.)
          I guess you could say we had a dif-
          ferent kind of education.

JEANNIE AND BILLY
run through the CLUB'S CATACOMBS. They open a door and find
a musician shooting up. Behind another door, a couple grabs
their clothes.

LATER - THE CLUB OFFICE

Jeannie lies awake on a makeshift bed. Billy's sleeping. The
trumpet solo from "I Can't Get Started," plays OVER. Jeannie
gets up and looks through the door.

Her father stands in the spotlight playing with such emotion, it sounds as though his trumpet is crying. It's a
moment that will always haunt her.

COPS BUST IN

SIRENS and LIGHTS blast on. Customers scramble for the side
doors. Jack rushes off the stage, grabs Billy and Jeannie,
and they hightail it out of there.

QUICK SHOTS - THE ROAD

-A CLUB before opening. Twelve-year-old Jeannie bangs on the
drums. Tries the horn. Blows on a reed. Jack, with a couple
of band members, emerges from a locked room.

-SCAT ROBBINS, the pianist shows Jeannie a few notes on the
keyboard.

-A YEAR LATER Jeannie plays for her dad. Jack is a man who holds back emotions, except on the horn. Jeannie looks up and sees him crying. He proudly applauds her. It is a defining moment. To her this means everything.

In the background, Billy is playing with a toy airplane.

> JEANNIE (V.O.)
> After Daddy died Billy joined the Navy and got as far away from music as he could. But for me, there was nothing else and no other place to go.

SUPERIMPOSED ON THE SCREEN:
1942, New York City

INT. THEATER - BROADWAY DISTRICT - DAY

Feminine hands at the piano play a swing blues progression.

GO BIGGER

Jeannie Jerome, now twenty-four, is auditioning for some male producers. She wears baggy pleated pants like the free wheeling spirited Hepburn and role models of her day.

With an impressive run, she slams down hard on the last chord. Her ability, like her and music, is sensational.

Total silence. Finally someone speaks.

> PRODUCER
> For a lady you're good.

> JEANNIE
> (incredulous)
> Excuse me?

> PRODUCER
> You ever hear of George Simon?

                         JEANNIE
            He's a music critic, what about him?

                             PRODUCER
            It's like George says, "Only God can make a
            tree. Only men can play good jazz."

                         JEANNIE
            Yeah? Well, George Simon is an ass!

A grey-haired man in his fifties quickly gets up. He is
ANDY ROBINSON.

                             ANDY
            Jeannie, . . .

                         JEANNIE
            No, Andy, . . .

                        JEANNIE (cont'd)
            My tunes were better then every one of the
            men that went before me and you know it!

We now see the five other composers in the audience. Andy
grabs Jeannie by the hand.

                        JEANNIE (cont'd)
            I'm not leaving!

She grabs her sheet music, flailing it.

                        JEANNIE (cont'd)
            You prejudiced, tone deaf, tin-eared,
            son of. . . .

Andy's hand covers her mouth. Jeannie yanks it away.

                      JEANNIE (V.O.) (cont'd)
            I'm reporting you to the ACLU.

Making Your Script Look the Way It Should

Writer's Resources—Standard Script Format—This is one take on the Standard Script Format. Please note that this script format aid originally appeared on *The Daily Script* under the webmaster Dana Franklin. Dana wrote this based upon the Warner Brothers formatting style. Dana no longer maintains the site. This appears here without his permission.

Learning the Correct Margins

Margins within Script

Script Type	Left Margin	Right Margin
Stage direction and	1.7"	1.1"
shot headings Dialog	2.7"	2.4"
Character names	4.1"	n/a
Parenthetical direction	3.4"	3.1"
within dialog		
Scenes transitions	6.0"	n/a
Scene/shot numbers	1.0"	7.4"

Top page margin is .5" (or three single lines) before the page number. A single blank line separates the page number from the body of the script, which begins with either a CONTINUED: or a new shot heading/slug line.

Bottom page margin is at least .5" (or three single lines) following the (CONTINUED) or the end of a scene.

Total page length is a maximum of sixty lines, including page number and CONTINUEDs (but not including the three line margins at the top and bottom of the page).

Paper size is 8.5" wide by 11" long.

Font

Use 12-point **Courier** (*not* Courier New) or Prestige Pica. These are fixed-pitch fonts that yield ten (10) characters per horizontal inch and six (6) lines per vertical inch.

Index